Play and Win Texas Hold 'Em

Belinda Levez

D0067052

A former betting shop manager, Belinda Levez is the author of numerous books on casino games and horse racing, including the Teach Yourself book *Back a Winning Horse*.

Play and Win Texas Hold 'Em

Belinda Levez

Also available in ebook

Contents

Introduction

This book explains the game of online Texas hold 'em poker. This gambling game is one of the most popular forms of poker played for real money. What makes Texas hold 'em so appealing is the way that a player's chances of winning or losing can dramatically change throughout the game with the turn of a card. It is also the game that is played to decide the World Series of Poker.

Playing online allows you the convenience of playing in your own home at a time that suits you. There is always a game on, no matter what time of the day or night. Many people find playing on the Internet less intimidating than playing in a casino. They can remain anonymous to the other players and are identified only by their pseudonyms. There is no need to worry about having a poker face.

Alternatively, it is possible to play live webcam poker. This gives a more realistic game reminiscent of private games, where you see the players. This allows you to get a more accurate assessment of the other players, as you can see their reactions to their hands and to the actions of the other players. It allows you to spot tells, as in a traditional game. It also means that the other players can see you and assess your reactions.

Online poker is cheaper than going to a bricks-and-mortar casino. The rake on an online site is often around 5 per cent, which is lower than in many casinos. In addition, you don't have to pay membership fees or travel costs.

There is a huge amount of competition for customers, which means tax-free betting, low commission rates, initial free bets and bonuses are all offered. It is therefore worth shopping around to find a good deal.

There are many elements to a Texas hold 'em game. To become a good player at Texas hold 'em you will need to master many skills. These include:

▶ playing at the correct level

▶ appreciating how good your hand is

- knowing when to play and when to fold
- being able to assess the other players correctly
- developing a correct betting strategy
- understanding the odds
- developing a good strategy for bluffing
- taking advantage of table position.

This book will take you step by step through the various aspects of the game. Starting with the basics about ranking of hands, it continues to expand your knowledge through to advanced strategies for playing. It will highlight the essentials about staying solvent, sticking to a budget and avoiding problem gambling. The calculation of odds is explained in an easy-to-understand way.

At the end of the course you should be more knowledgeable about the game and have useful insights to make you a better player.

Abbreviations are used for some terms:

A – ace	s – spades
K – king	d – diamonds
Q – queen	c – clubs
h – hearts	

When carrying out the exercises in the book, it will help to have a pack of cards so that you can lay out the various hands. This will help you to better visualize the hands. For the betting examples, you may find it helpful to visualize them using chips or coins.

1

The basics

In this chapter you will learn:

▶ *The aim of poker*
▶ *The basic game*
▶ *The ranking of hands*
▶ *Which hand wins at a showdown*
▶ *How to learn the rankings*
▶ *Tips for quickly identifying the hand.*

The aim of poker

Poker is a gambling card game where the aim is to win the pot by having the highest-ranking hand. A poker hand is made up of five cards. Different combinations of cards are ranked according to the chances of acquiring a particular hand. The odds of being dealt some hands are greater than others. The more difficult a hand is to achieve, the higher its position is in the ranking. Figure 1.1 shows the names of the hands and how the hands are ranked.

Players bet on their hands and contribute to a pot of money which they try to win. The pot is the total amount of money that has been bet on the game. Poker is made more interesting as players may bluff – that is, give the impression that they have a good hand when in fact they have a poor hand. In this way players with a poor hand also have a chance of winning the pot. Throughout the game there are rounds of betting. Players are able to increase the amount bet, to try to force other players out of the game. A successful player forces the other players to concede and wins the pot.

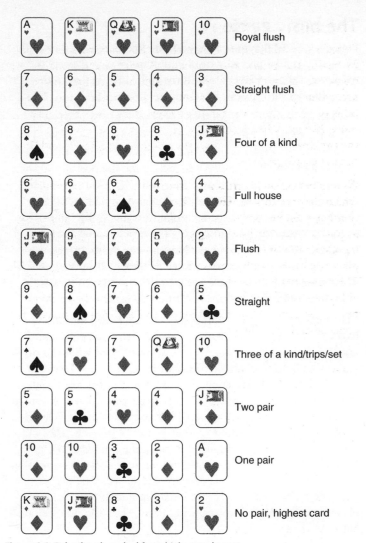

Figure 1.1 Poker hands ranked from highest to lowest

The basic game

One deck of 52 playing cards with the jokers removed is used. The game can be played with a minimum of two players and a maximum of ten. Players take turns to be the 'dealer', although he or she does not physically deal the cards.

Players are 'seated' around a virtual card table. A marker called the dealer button denotes the position of the dealer. The position of the dealer is indicated, as this determines the order of play and who bets first. After each game the position of the dealer moves one player clockwise. Before any cards are dealt, the two players to the ~~right~~ left of the dealer make an initial bet, called the big blind and the small blind respectively. This helps to increase the pot. The amount bet will depend on the rules of the game. It also makes the game more competitive as players are more likely to try to win the pot if they have contributed to it. Bets are made with chips (counters that represent particular denominations of money).

The cards are dealt in several stages. Players are initially dealt two cards. These two cards are personal to each player and are seen only by him. The players do not know what the other players have been dealt. A round of betting takes place. A further three cards are dealt face up. These cards are visible to all players. A further round of betting takes place. A fourth card is dealt face up. A round of betting takes place. A final card is dealt face up and a further round of betting takes place. If only one player is remaining in the game, he wins the pot. If there are two or more players remaining, a showdown takes place. The hands of the players are compared. The player with the highest-ranking hand wins the pot. If two or more players tie for the highest-ranking hand, then the pot is shared between them.

Players have several options during the course of the game: they can fold, check, bet or raise.

1 **Folding** Folding is withdrawing from the game and taking no further part. This gives players the opportunity to stop playing if they have a poor hand or if the betting is at a high level. Suppose you are dealt a poor hand or you fail to

improve on your hand, you may decide that it is not worth continuing to play. It is possible to fold at any point during the game. When it is your turn to play you simply click on the fold button. Any money that you have contributed to the pot will be lost. The remaining players then continue to play until the pot is won. If you are the only player remaining after all the other players have folded, then you will win the pot.

2 **Checking** It is only possible to 'check' (not bet or pass) when no one has bet during the betting round. Players who decide to check do not contribute any money to the pot. The action then passes to the next person. If someone then bets, the person who checked must contribute the same amount of money to the pot to stay in the game. If everyone checks in a betting round, then that round of betting is complete.

3 **Betting** At each stage of the game players bet an amount of money that is contributed to the pot. The rules of the specific game will determine how much must be bet at each stage. Some bets are forced bets, like the small blind and big blind, which must be made before any cards are dealt. Players take it in turns to make these bets.

Once the cards have been dealt, the players take turns to bet. The first bet determines how much each player has to bet in order to stay in the game. Betting continues clockwise around the table. Each subsequent player must bet at least as much as the previous player to stay in the game.

Depending on the rules of the game, the betting can be organized in different ways. Chapter 3 deals with the different ways of betting.

4 **Raising** Players may also increase the amount bet. If a player raises then the subsequent players must match the amount raised in order to stay in the game. The amount of the raise will depend on the game rules.

GOING ALL-IN
Going all-in is betting all of your remaining chips. This can occur when you are low on chips and do not have enough to continue the game to the end. When a player goes all-in they

have the chance to win the pot that they have so far contributed to. A second pot is then started that will contain the subsequent bets. The remaining players continue playing and compete for both the first and second pots. It is also possible for other players to go all-in, thus creating a third pot and so on. At a showdown the other players' cards will be compared to those of the all-in player for the first pot and then the remaining players' cards will be compared for the second pot. In no-limit games it is common for players to go all-in, as the rules allow for unlimited bets.

THE SHOWDOWN

If all remaining players have matched the last bet and there are no further raises, a showdown occurs. The players' cards are revealed. The hands of the players are then compared. The player with the highest-ranking poker hand wins the pot. In the event of a tie the pot is shared.

The ranking of hands

A poker hand is made from five cards. A hand is named according to what cards it contains. The hands are named as follows:

- Royal flush
- Straight flush
- Four of a kind
- Full house
- Flush

- Straight
- Three of a kind/trips/set
- Two pair
- One pair
- No pair, highest card

The hands are ranked in a set order (see Figure 1.1). The more difficult a hand is to achieve, the higher its ranking. Each type of hand is also ranked according to the values of the cards. The highest-value cards are aces and the lowest are 2s. The cards are ranked in the following descending order:

A, K, Q, J, 10, 9, 8, 7, 6, 5, 4, 3, 2

The suits do not affect the ranking, so if two players have an identical hand, one with hearts and one with spades, the hands will tie. In straights, the ace can also be used as a low card (see below).

ROYAL FLUSH

The highest-ranking hand is a royal flush – A, K, Q, J, 10 in the same suit. There are only four ways that this hand can be made, with hearts, diamonds, spades or clubs. If you are dealt this hand, you know that you have the highest-ranking hand and you are very unlikely to be beaten by any other player. The only other possibility is that another player may also have a royal flush and therefore tie with you.

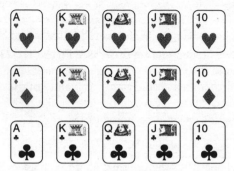

Figure 1.2a Example hands featuring a royal flush

STRAIGHT FLUSH

A straight flush is a run of five cards in numerical order of the same suit in consecutive numerical order. Note: a royal flush is also a straight flush.

If two players both have a straight flush, the player with the highest card wins, so Kc, Qc, Jc, 10c, 9c beats Qh, Jh, 10h, 9h, 8h. If two players both have the same straight flush with different suits, the hand is a tie and the pot is shared. Jc, 10c, 9c, 8c, 7c ties with Js, 10s, 9s, 8s, 7s. The lowest straight flush is 5c, 4c, 3c, 2c, Ac. In this case the ace is a low card. It is not possible to have a straight flush where the ace is anything other than high or low. So 4c, 3c, 2c, Ac, Kc is not a valid hand.

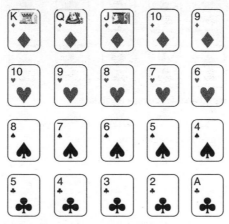

Figure 1.2b Example hands featuring a straight flush

FOUR OF A KIND

Four of a kind is four cards of the same numerical value with any other card. Four aces is the highest-ranking four of a kind and will beat four kings. Where two players both have a four of kind, the hand with the highest value for the four of a kind wins. Thus:

► A, A, A, A, J would beat K, K, K, K, Q.

► 10, 10, 10, 10, K would beat 8, 8, 8, 8, A.

► Q, Q, Q, Q, K would beat J, J, J, J, 10.

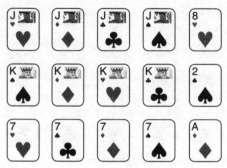

Figure 1.2c Example hands featuring four of a kind

FULL HOUSE

A full house is three of a kind (three cards of the same value) with a pair (two cards of the same value). Where two players have a full house, the hand with the highest value for the three of a kind wins. Thus:

▶ 10, 10, 10, 2, 2 would beat 8, 8, 8, K, K.

▶ 4, 4, 4, 10, 10 would beat 2, 2, 2, A, A.

▶ Q, Q, Q, 7, 7 would beat 10, 10, 10, 5, 5.

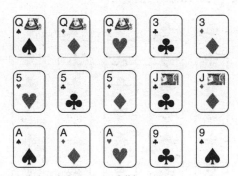

Figure 1.2d Example hands featuring a full house

FLUSH

A flush is five cards of the same suit in any numerical order. Where two players have a flush, the one with the highest card wins. Thus:

▶ Js, 8s, 6s, 5s, 3s would beat 9d, 8d, 6d, 5d, 4d.

▶ Ac, Jc, 7c, 4c, 3c would beat Kc, Qc, 10c, 9c, 8c.

▶ 8d, 6d, 4d, 3d, 2d would beat 7h, 5h, 4h, 3h, 2h.

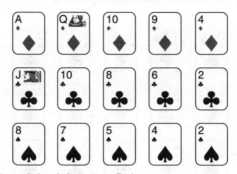

Figure 1.2e Example hands featuring a flush

STRAIGHT

A straight is five cards of any suit in consecutive numerical order. A, K, Q, J, 10 is the highest straight followed by K, Q, J, 10, 9. Where two players both have a straight, the hand with the highest card wins:

▶ Qh, Jc, 10d, 9s, 8c would beat Jd, 10c, 9h, 8d, 7s.

▶ Ad, Kh, Js, 10d, 9c would beat Qh, Js, 10h, 9h, 8d.

▶ 10d, 9d, 8d, 7c, 6c would beat 8h, 7h, 6c, 5d, 4h.

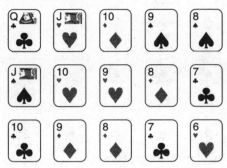

Figure 1.2f Example hands featuring a straight

THREE OF A KIND/TRIPS/SET

Three of a kind, also known as a trips or a set, is three cards of the same numerical value with two other cards. Where two players both have a three of a kind, the hand with the highest three of a kind wins:

▶ 6h, 6d, 6c, 8h, 5d would beat 4d, 4s, 4c, Ad, Kh.

▶ Ac, Ad, Ah, 3h, 2c would beat 10d, 10h, 10c, As, Ks.

▶ Js, Jh, Jd, Kh, Jh would beat 8h, 8d, 8c, Ad, 3h.

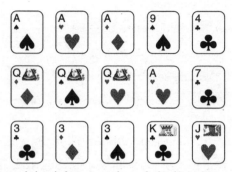

Figure 1.2g Example hands featuring a three of a kind/trips/set

TWO PAIR

Two pair is two sets of pairs (two cards with the same value) with any other card. Where two players both have two pair, the value of the highest pair decides the winner:

▶ A, A, 3, 3, 2 would beat 10, 10, 8, 8, A.

▶ J, J, 9, 9, A would beat 9, 9, 7, 7, A.

▶ K, K, 2, 2, 3 would beat 7, 7, 6, 6, K.

If both players have the same two pair, the value of the fifth card decides the winner:

▶ K, K, Q, Q, 8 would beat K, K, Q, Q, 4.

▶ A, A, J, J, 4 would beat A, A, J, J, 3.

▶ 9, 9, 8, 8, 5 would beat 9, 9, 8, 8, 4.

If two players both have cards with the same value, there is a tie and the pot is shared:

▶ Ad, Ac, Jc, Jh, 9d ties with Ah, As, Js, Jd, 9s.

▶ Kd, Kh, 10s, 10c, 7h ties with Kc, Ks, 10h, 10d, 7s.

▶ 10c, 10h, 8d, 8c, 5s ties with 10d, 10s, 8s, 8h, 5c.

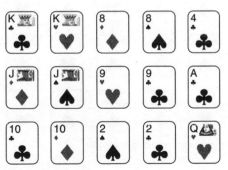

Figure 1.2h Example hands featuring a two pair

ONE PAIR

One pair is two cards of the same value with three other cards of different values:

▶ A, A, 10, 4, 2 would beat K, K, A, 10, 4.

▶ Q, Q, 8, 7, 3 would beat J, J, K, 10, 9.

▶ 10, 10, 5, 3, 2 would beat 9, 9, A, K, 7.

If two players have the same pair, the hand with the highest-value other cards wins:

▶ A, A, 10, 7, 5 would beat A, A, 9, 7, 5.

▶ K, K, A, 6, 2 would beat K, K, A, 4, 2.

▶ 9, 9, K, 7, 4 would beat 9, 9, K, 7, 3.

If all of the cards are of the same value then there is a tie:

▶ Kd, Kc, 9c, 8s, 7d ties with Kc, Kh, 9d, 8d, 7s.

▶ Ah, As, 10d, 9h, 7h ties with Ad, Ac, 10h, 9s, 7s.

▶ 7s, 7h, Ah, Kd, 3c ties with 7c, 7d, As, Kh, 3d.

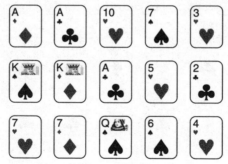

Figure 1.2i Example hands featuring a one pair

HIGHEST CARD

Where none of the named ranking hands is held, the winner is the player with the highest card. In a showdown a hand containing an ace would beat one with a king and so on. Qh, 10h, 7d, 3s, 2c would beat Jd, 10s, 4c, 3h, 2s.

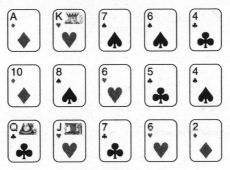

Figure 1.2j Example hands featuring a highest card

Questions to ask yourself

Because games are played at a fast pace online, it is crucially important that you can quickly determine what hand you have. The cards are laid out in the order that they are dealt, so it is not always easy to immediately identify the highest hand. Ask yourself:

▶ Are any cards of the same numerical value?

▶ If yes, consider if the hand contains a pair, two pair, three of a kind, four of a kind or a full house.

▶ Are the cards consecutive numbers?

▶ If yes, consider if the hand contains a royal flush, a straight flush or a straight.

▶ Are the cards the same suit?

▶ If yes, the hand is a flush. You should take particular care to look out for flushes because they can be the easiest hands to miss as at first they may seem of little value as they can be made from low cards.

Which hand wins at a showdown?

If there are two or more players still in the game when all the betting rounds have been completed, then the players' hands are compared. The one with the highest-ranking hand wins.

EXAMPLE 1

Player a is the winner. Both players have a full house, but player a has the highest value for the three of a kind.

EXAMPLE 2

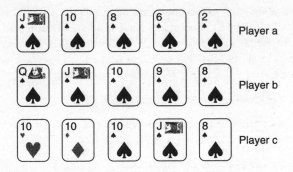

Player b is the winner with a straight flush. Player a has a flush and player c has three of a kind – both of which are lower-ranking hands than a straight flush.

EXAMPLE 3

Player c is the winner with a flush. Player a has three of a kind with aces and player b has a straight, both of which are lower-ranking hands than a flush.

EXAMPLE 4

Player a is the winner with a full house of kings over queens.
Player b has three of a kind with kings. Player c has two pair
with kings and queens. Three of a kind and two pair both rank
lower than a full house.

Try it now: How to learn the rankings

You need to get lots of practice identifying hands. Take a pack of cards
and deal out four five-card hands. Determine the name of each hand
and then put them in order. Check against Figure 1.1 to make sure that
they are correct. Continue to practise until you easily recognize what the
ranking is.

Test your knowledge (answers at the back)

What is the name of each of the following hands?

1 Jc, 8d, 9d, Kh, Jd

2 Ad, Qd, 10d, Jd, Kd

3 8d, 8h, 8c, 10h, 8s

4 3c, Qc, 10c, 7c, Kc

5 Kd, 10h, Ac, 8d, Qs

6   10h, 5d, 10d, 5s, 8h

7   Kd, Qh, Ks, Qc, Kc

8   10s, 7d, 8h, Jc, 9c

9   Qs, Qd, Kc, Qh, Jd

10   2d, 5d, Ad, 4d, 3d

Compare the following hands. Which one would win a showdown?

11   a 4d, 7d, Kd, Ad, Qd

    b Ah, Kd, 7d, Kh, Ks

12   a 8h, Kc, 7c, Ks, Ad

    b 10d, 4s, 9c, 4d, 10h

13   a 7c, 10s, 9d, 8s, Jh

    b Qc, Kc, Qh, Ks, Qd

14   a 10h, Ah, Qh, Kh, Jh

    b 9h, Qh, Ah, Jh, 10h

15   a 7d, 10d, 6d, 9d, 8d

    b 10d, 7d, 10h, 7c, 10s

16   a 8d, Jd, 9d, 7d, 10d

    b 7d, 10h, 8d, Jd, 9d

17   a Js, Kd, Jh, As, Jc

    b As, Kd, Jh, Ah, Kc

18   a Jh, 8s, 10c, 6d, Kd

    b 6d, Jh, 10c, Qd, 8s

19   a Qc, Jh, Qs, 10c, Qd

    b 10c, Qd, 8s, Jh, 9d

20   a 7d, Ah, 7h, 7c, 7s

    b Ah, Kd, Ac, Kh, As

Next step

You have now learned the basics of poker. You should be able to easily recognize what hand you have and where it comes in the ranking. In a showdown you should be able to quickly work out which hand has won. In the next chapter you will learn how Texas hold 'em is played.

2

Introducing Texas hold 'em

In this chapter you will learn:

- ▶ *The aim of Texas hold 'em*
- ▶ *The basic game*
- ▶ *How a hand is made*
- ▶ *About nuts*
- ▶ *How a hand changes as the game progresses*
- ▶ *How to decide the winner*
- ▶ *About split pot*
- ▶ *Some examples of step-by-step games.*

The aim of Texas hold 'em

The aim of Texas hold 'em is to win the pot by making the highest-ranking poker hand from any combination of the cards in the player's hand and the cards laid out on the table. The player's hand consists of two cards, and there are five community cards face up on the table.

What sets Texas hold 'em apart from other games of poker is that a player's fortunes can dramatically change throughout the game. The cards are dealt in stages, so that a player can see a hand that initially showed great promise become worthless or, alternatively, can see what initially seemed a worthless hand win. Sometimes, it is even possible to know that you have the best possible hand and that none of the other players can beat you.

The basic game

Texas hold 'em is a variant of stud poker. In stud poker games some cards are placed face up on the table. These cards are community cards and are available for all players to use in their hands. The community cards are referred to as the board. Players are also dealt personal cards that only they see. These are called pocket cards or hole cards.

With Texas hold 'em the player receives two pocket cards and five community cards are placed face up on the table. The players then use any of the seven cards to make a five-card poker hand.

There are ten stages to a Texas hold 'em game, as follows:

1 The blind bets

2 Dealing the pocket cards

3 A round of betting

4 Dealing the flop

5 A round of betting

6 Dealing the turn

7 A round of betting

8 Dealing the river

9 A round of betting

10 The showdown.

THE BLIND BETS

A marker denotes the position of the dealer. This is usually a circle marked with a D (dealer). The players do not deal the cards as this role is taken by the computer. The position of the dealer is important as it determines who places the initial bets and who goes first in each round of betting. After each game the position of the dealer moves one place clockwise around the table. Each game of hold 'em starts with the placing of the blind bets before the dealing of the cards. The movement of the dealer button after each game ensures that each player takes a turn at contributing to the blind bets. There are two blind bets: the small blind and the big blind. The big blind is double the value of the small blind. So, if the small blind is £1, the big blind is £2. The moving of the dealer button after each game also allows each player to have the chance of acting first and last in the betting. This helps to even out the advantages that are gained by acting last in the betting.

HOW THE CARDS ARE DEALT

The cards are dealt in stages with betting rounds in between. The actions that the players can take during the betting rounds are fold, check, bet, call and raise. There are a number of different ways in which the betting can be arranged. This is shown in detail in Chapter 3.

POCKET CARDS

The first two cards dealt to each player are called the pocket cards or hole cards. These cards are personal to each player. The other players do not see your pocket cards, and you do not see the other players' pocket cards until the showdown is reached. Based on these cards, players decide whether or not to stay in the game. If a player decides to fold, their pocket cards are discarded and are not shown to the other players. If, however, the game ends in a showdown, then the pocket cards can be seen.

THE COMMUNITY CARDS

The next cards to be dealt are the community cards in three stages:

1 **The flop** Three community cards are dealt face up on the table. Everyone sees these cards and they can be used by everyone.

2 **The turn** A fourth card is dealt face up on the table.

3 **The river** A fifth and final card is dealt face up on the table.

The community cards are often referred to as the board.

THE SHOWDOWN

When betting is finished, the hands of the remaining players are compared. The player with the highest-ranking poker hand wins. If there is a tie, the pot is divided between the number of players in the tie. If there is only one player left at the end of the game because all the other players have folded, no showdown takes place. He wins the pot without revealing his cards.

How a hand is made

A Texas hold 'em hand is a five-card hand made from any of the two pocket cards and the five community cards. This gives you a total of seven cards from which to make a hand. Your hand is the highest possible ranking hand made from this combination. Examples a–j in Figure 2.1 below show how a hand is made.

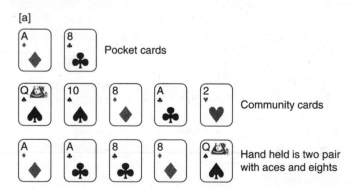

[a]

A♦ 8♣ — Pocket cards

Q♠ 10♠ 8♦ A♣ 2♥ — Community cards

A♦ A♣ 8♣ 8♦ Q♠ — Hand held is two pair with aces and eights

[b]

K♦ 10♥ Pocket cards

J♦ 9♣ 2♥ Q♠ 8♦ Community cards

K♦ Q♠ J♦ 10♥ 9♣ Hand held is a straight

[c]

A♦ 6♥ Pocket cards

A♠ 4♣ A♣ 3♦ J♥ Community cards

A♦ A♠ A♣ J♥ 6♥ Hand held is three of a kind with aces

[d]

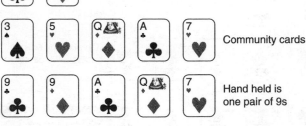

9♣ 9♦ Pocket cards

3♠ 5♥ Q♦ A♣ 7♥ Community cards

9♣ 9♦ A♣ Q♦ 7♥ Hand held is one pair of 9s

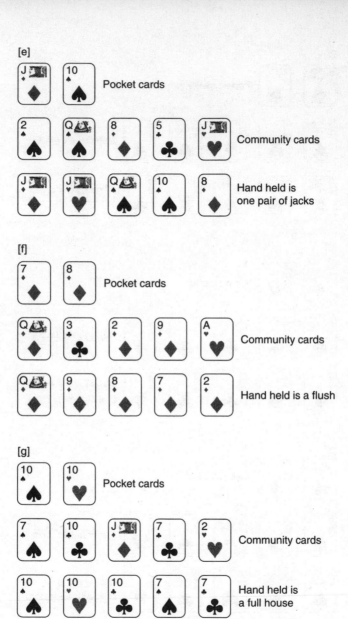

[e]

J♦ 10♠ Pocket cards

2♠ Q♠ 8♦ 5♣ J♥ Community cards

J♦ J♥ Q♠ 10♠ 8♦ Hand held is one pair of jacks

[f]

7♦ 8♦ Pocket cards

Q♦ 3♣ 2♦ 9♦ A♥ Community cards

Q♦ 9♦ 8♦ 7♦ 2♦ Hand held is a flush

[g]

10♠ 10♥ Pocket cards

7♠ 10♣ J♦ 7♣ 2♥ Community cards

10♠ 10♥ 10♣ 7♠ 7♣ Hand held is a full house

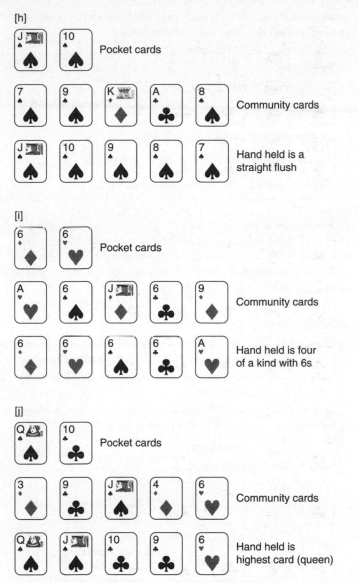

Figure 2.1 How a hand is made

Sometimes there will be a high-ranking hand in the community cards. This hand can be used by everyone:

Example

Pocket cards player a: 10h, 10s

Pocket cards player b: Jc, Jd

Community cards: Ah, Ac, Ad, Ks, Kd

Players a's hand is a full house: Ah, Ac, Ad, Ks, Kd.

Player b's hand is a full house: Ah, Ac, Ad, Ks, Kd

In a showdown, player a's and b's hands tie and they will share the pot. The fact that player b's pocket cards are higher than player a's makes no difference to the winning hand. All of the other players who folded have lost, even though they could have shared the pot by staying in the game.

Nuts

In Texas hold 'em large number of the cards that can potentially be used to make up a hand are visible. This means that occasionally you may know that you have the best possible hand. You can see that it is impossible for another player to beat you. This is called nuts. Sometimes this can happen after the flop. At other times, you may need to wait to see all of the community cards.

Let's look at some examples:

EXAMPLE 1

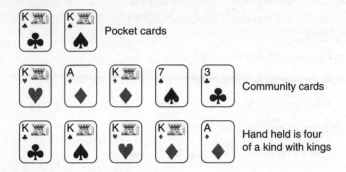

Pocket cards

Community cards

Hand held is four
of a kind with kings

In this example the player's hand is four of a kind with four
kings – Kc, Ks, Kh, Kd, Ad. It is a hand that cannot be beaten.
Only four aces or a straight flush could beat this hand. It is
impossible for another player to have four aces as only one
is showing on the board. If another player has two aces, the
maximum hand that that player could have is three of a kind.
A straight flush is also not possible. A player with Qd, Jd pocket
cards does not have the ten to complete a royal flush.

EXAMPLE 2

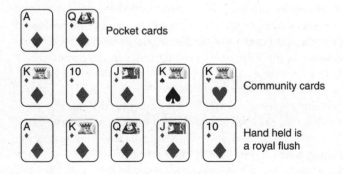

Pocket cards

Community cards

Hand held is
a royal flush

Here the player has a royal flush – Ad, Kd, Qd, Jd, 10d – and knows by the flop that he has the highest hand and that it cannot be beaten. The highest hand that another player could have is four of a kind with kings.

EXAMPLE 3

Occasionally, two or more players may have the nuts and will tie in a showdown:

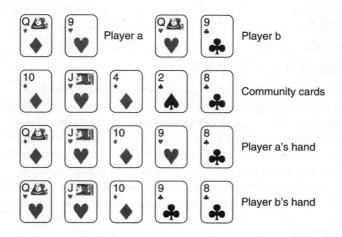

Both player a's and b's pocket cards have the same value. Player a's hand is a straight Qd, Jh, 10d, 9h, 8c. It can't be beaten by a flush as it is not possible for another player to have five diamonds as there are only two diamonds in the community cards. A full house or four of a kind is not possible. The only possibility is that there could be a tie for the hand if another player has a queen and a 9. In this case, player b has the same straight – Qh, Jh, 10d, 9c, 8c. If they both remain in the game to the showdown, they will share the pot. It would be possible for up to four players to have the same hand if they were each dealt a queen and a 9 in their pocket cards.

How a hand changes as the game progresses

As the game progresses, the value of a hand can change. Being initially dealt good pocket cards may give the impression that you have a great hand. However, you may not improve your hand on the flop. A pair of aces, for example, looks less useful if in the flop Q, Q, K are dealt. Although you now have a two pair, there is the likelihood of someone being able to beat you with three or four queens or three kings.

Deciding the winner

If during the game all the other players have folded and only one player remains, then he will win the pot. Since the players may fold at any stage of the game, it is possible to get a winner at any stage. For example: after the pocket cards have been dealt, all but one player could fold. The remaining player will win the pot and no further cards will be dealt. The hands of players who fold are not shown to the other players. If there are two or more players remaining at the end of the game there will be a showdown. Their hands are compared and the highest-ranking hand wins.

EXAMPLE 1

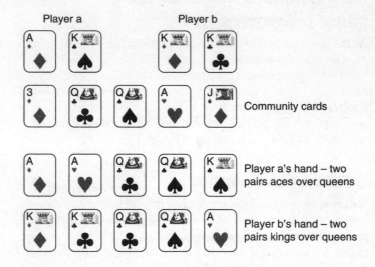

Player a's hand is two pair aces over queens: A, A, Q, Q, K.
Player b's hand is two pair kings over queens: K, K, Q, Q, A.
Player a wins the showdown.

EXAMPLE 2

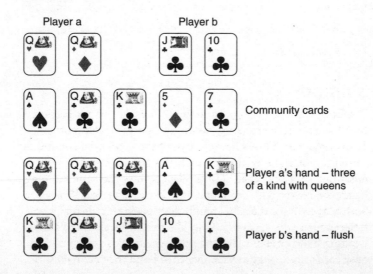

Player a's hand is three of a kind with queens: Qh, Qd, Qc, As, Kc.

Player b's hand is a flush with clubs: Kc, Qc, Jc, 10c, 7c.

Player b wins the showdown.

EXAMPLE 3

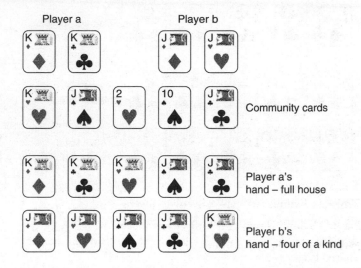

Player a's hand is a full house kings over jacks: Kd, Kc, Kh, Js, Jc.

Player b's hand is four of a kind with jacks: Jd, Jh, Js, Jc, Kh.

Player b wins the showdown.

Split pot

A split pot is when two or more players share the pot because they have the same ranking hand. Split pots are common in Texas hold 'em. This is because five of the cards (the community cards) can be used by any player. It is a common misconception regarding split pots that, if both players have the same ranking hand, the player with the highest pocket cards wins. When both players have the same hand, their pocket cards make no difference to who has won. Only the five cards that make the winning hand count. All of the other cards are irrelevant. The only cards that count are the five-card hand that he makes.

EXAMPLE 1

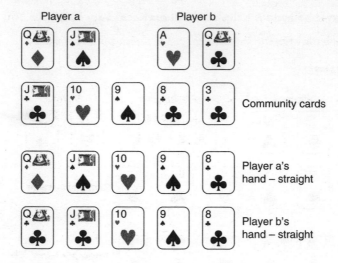

Player a's hand is a straight Qd, Js, 10h, 9s, 8c.

Player b's hand is a straight Qc, Jc, 10h, 9s, 8c.

As both players have the same hand, the hands tie so the pot is shared between players a and b.

EXAMPLE 2

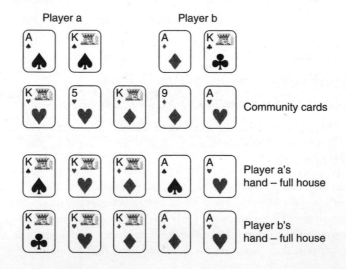

Player a's hand is a full house kings over aces: Ks, Kh, Kd, As, Ah.

Player b's hand is a full house kings over aces: Kc, Kh, Kd, Ad, Ah.

The hands tie, so the pot is shared between players a and b.

EXAMPLE 3

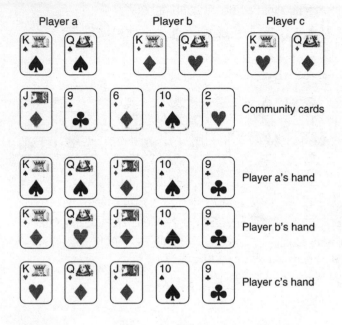

Player a's hand is a straight Ks, Qs, Jd, 10s, 9c.

Player b's hand is a straight Kd, Qh, Jd, 10s, 9c.

Player c's hand is a straight Kh, Qd, Jd, 10s, 9c.

All three players have the same hand (the different suits make no difference). The showdown is a tie. Each player wins one-third of the pot.

Step-by-step games

EXAMPLE 1

There are five players a, b, c, d and e. Player a is the dealer.

The blinds:

> Player b makes the small blind (£1).

> Player c makes the big blind (£2).

Dealing of the pocket cards. The first two cards are dealt face down to each player:

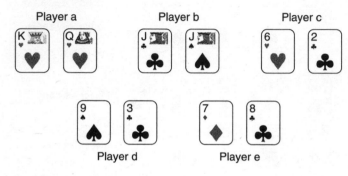

Player a	Player b	Player c

Player d   Player e

> Player a – Kh, Qh

> Player b – Jc, Js

> Player c – 6h, 2c

> Player d – 9s, 3c

> Player e – 7d, 8c

Player d goes first and bets. The betting continues clockwise around the table until all players have contributed the same amount to the pot.

> Player e folds.

> Player a calls.

> Player b raises.

Player c folds.

Player d calls.

Player a calls.

The remaining players have now matched player b's raise.

The flop is dealt. The community cards are: Kd, Jh, 3d.

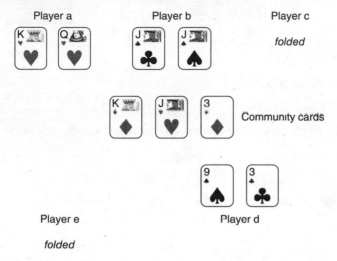

Player a   Player b   Player c

folded

Community cards

Player e   Player d

folded

Betting now starts to the left of the dealer:

Player b goes first – he raises.

Player d folds.

Player b calls.

The turn is dealt. The community cards are: Kd, Jh, 3d, 9h.

Community cards

Player b bets.

Player a calls.

The river is dealt. The community cards are: Kd, Jh, 3d, 9h, 5s.

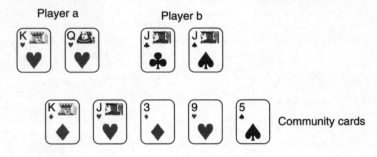

Community cards

Player b bets.

Player a folds.

Player b wins the pot.

As there is only one player remaining, he wins the pot. He does not reveal his cards to the other players.

EXAMPLE 2

The dealer button moves one place to the left. Player b is now the dealer.

The blind bets are made. Player c makes the small blind bet and player d makes the big blind bet.

The pocket cards are dealt. Player a has Ks, Qs; player b has 9c, 6h; player c has As, Qh; and player d has Qd, Jd.

The first betting round commences. Player a is the first to act. He bets. Player b folds. Player c calls the bet. Player d calls.

The flop is dealt. The community cards are now 7d, 5d, Ah.

Community cards

The second betting round commences. Player c is the first to act. He now has a pair of aces. He bets. Player d has four cards to a flush. He raises. Player a has failed to improve. He folds.

The turn is dealt. The community cards are now 7d, 5d, Ah, Qc.

[c]

Community cards

Player c is the first to act. He now has two pair aces over queens. He raises. Player d still has four cards to a flush. He calls.

The river is dealt. The community cards are now 7d, 5d, Ah, Qc, 4d.

[d]

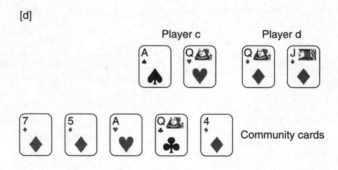

Community cards

Player c is the first to act. He bets. Player d now has a flush. He raises. Player c calls.

At the showdown player c has a two pair: As, Ah, Qh, Qc, 7d. Player d has a flush: Qd, Jd, 7d, 5d, 4d. Player d has the highest-ranking hand and wins the pot. As two players reached the showdown, their pocket cards are revealed to the other players.

Test your knowledge (answers at the back)

What hand does the player have?

1 Pocket cards: Kh, Kc

   Community cards: 5s, 9d, As, Jc, Qd

2 Pocket cards: Qd, 10c

   Community cards: 7h, Js, 9d, 8c, 3c

3 Pocket cards: Jh, Jd

   Community cards: 10s, Jc, 10h, Js, 10c

4 Pocket cards: Ah, 10h

   Community cards: 7h, Ad, As, 4h, 9h

5 Pocket cards: Kd, Qd

   Community cards: 8s, Ks, 2d, 4h, Qc

6 Pocket cards: Ac, Jc

   Community cards: 10c, Qc, Js, Kc, Jh

7 Pocket cards: Qc, Js

   Community cards: Qd, 4d, Qs, Ah, 10c,

8 Pocket cards: Qc, 10d

   Community cards: Jd, 9h, 7h, 2c, 4s

9 Pocket cards Kd, 9d

   Community cards 7d, 10d, 6d, Kh, 8d

10 Pocket cards Jc, Jd

   Community cards: 10s, Qd, Jh, 10c, 9d

Which hand wins the showdown?

1 Player a: Ac, 10s

   Player b: Kh, 6h

   Community cards: Ad, Kc, Ah, 6c, 6d

2 Player a: Kc, Kh

Player b: 10s, 8s

Community cards: 9d, 7s, 5s, Kd, 6s

3 Player a: Qs, Ks

Player b: Ac, Ad

Community cards: Js, Kc, 8d, Qc, 5d

4 Player a: Ks, 9c

Player b: Jc, Js

Community cards: 5d, Jh, 10s, Qc, Jd

5 Player a: Qd, 10d

Player b: Ad, 7d

Community cards: Jd, Ac, Kd, 9d, As

6 Player a: Ad, Jc

Player b: Ac, Jh

Community cards: Js, 4c, Qh, Jd, Kc

7 Player a: Kd, Qd

Player b: Ac, Kh

Player c: Ks, Kc

Community cards: 10s, Ad, Qh, Jd, 3s

8 Player a: Kc, Ks

Player b: Jc, Js

Player c: Qh, Qc

Community cards: Jd, 8d, Qd, 9d, 10d

9 Player a: Kc, Qd

Player b: Qc, Jh

Player c: Ks, Kh

Community cards: Ah, As, Qd, Ad, Ac

10 Player a: 10d, 9s

Player b: Ks, Kh

Player c: 8c, 7h

Community cards: 10s, 9c, 5h, 6d, 8d, 7s

Next step

You should now have an understanding of how the cards are dealt, how to make a hand and what hand wins at a showdown. In the next chapter you will learn how the betting is organized. You will learn different methods of betting and how to calculate bets at each stage of the game.

3

Betting

In this chapter you will learn:

- ► *Basic betting terms*
- ► *Betting rounds*
- ► *The position of the dealer*
- ► *The blind bets*
- ► *About type of game and betting minimums*
- ► *Betting in fixed-limit, pot-limit and no-limit games.*

Betting terms

Betting is organized in several different ways. The main systems are fixed-limit, pot-limit and no-limit. The names are often abbreviated:

- ▶ Fixed-limit – FL

- ▶ Pot-limit – PL

- ▶ No-limit – NL

The fixed-limit games are predictable: you know how much the minimum and maximum bets are. With pot-limit and no-limit games the stakes can very quickly get very high. As a beginner, you should start out playing fixed-limit. The pot-limit and no-limit games should be tried only once you have plenty of experience. Before playing it is always advisable to check the rules, as different sites may vary.

Betting rounds

The betting is divided up into rounds. A round of betting takes place after the cards are dealt. The first round is after the pocket cards are dealt, the second after the flop, the third after the turn and the last after the river. For a player to remain in the game, they must bet an amount equal to the largest bet in each round. If they no longer want to remain in the game, they can fold when it is their turn to act. All money contributed to the pot before they fold will be lost.

During each round the chips contributed to the pot are shown in front of each player. This makes it easy to see how much each player has contributed so far and makes it easy to calculate how much the next player has to add to call a bet. A betting round ends when everyone who has not folded has contributed the same amount of money to the pot and there are no further raises. A running total of the pot is shown. When the betting round ends these chips are added to the pot.

Remember this: The rake

A rake/commission will be deducted from the pot. This is the amount that the poker site charges for its services. It will vary from between 1 per cent to 5 per cent of the stakes. The higher the stakes, the lower the rake. When playing online this will happen automatically as the chips are added to the pot. You will not need to calculate this amount while playing. To simplify the calculations, the examples here are shown without the rake being deducted.

The position of the dealer

The seats are numbered from 1 up to a maximum of 10. At the start of play, the player in seat 1 is the dealer. In the next game the dealer button moves one place to the left and the player in seat 2 is the dealer. After this game the dealer button moves one place to the left and the player in seat 3 takes a turn at being the dealer and so on.

The position of the dealer determines who bets first and who places the blind bets:

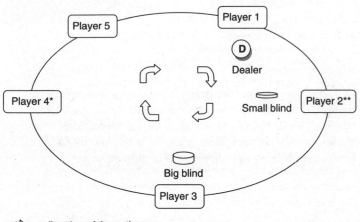

direction of the action
* first to act in the first betting round
** first to act in subsequent betting rounds

With five players in the first game, player 1 is the dealer. Player 2 makes the small blind and player 3 makes the big blind. After the pocket cards have been dealt, player 4 is the first to act. In all subsequent betting rounds player 2 is the first to act.

In the next game the dealer button moves one place to the left so that player 2 becomes the dealer. Player 3 makes the small blind and player 4 makes the big blind. After the pocket cards have been dealt, player 5 is the first to act. In all subsequent betting rounds player 3 is the first to act.

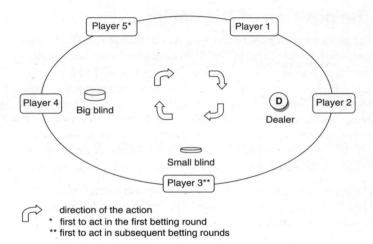

direction of the action
* first to act in the first betting round
** first to act in subsequent betting rounds

In the following game the dealer button moves one place to the left so that player 3 becomes the dealer. Player 4 makes the small blind and player 5 makes the big blind. After the pocket cards have been dealt, player 1 is the first to act. In all subsequent betting rounds player 4 is the first to act.

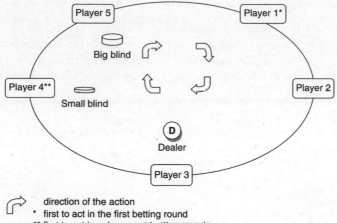

direction of the action
* first to act in the first betting round
** first to act in subsequent betting rounds

The blind bets

Blind bets are common to all forms of hold 'em. They ensure that every game has at least some money in the pot. The general idea is to increase the competition for the pot as players who have already contributed some money will want to try to win it back.

There are two blind bets – the big blind and the small blind. The blind bets are fixed amounts. The big blind is double the amount of the small blind.

The blind bets are placed before any cards are dealt. The player to the left of the dealer makes the small blind and the next player makes the big blind. After the pocket cards have been dealt, the first round of betting takes place. Everyone who has not folded must have contributed the same amount of money to the pot at the end of the betting round.

Example

If the small blind is £1 and the big blind is £2, and the other players bet the minimum bet of £2, when the betting reaches the small blind, in order to stay in the game, the small blind must make a bet of at least £1 so that all the other bets have been matched. If the small blind instead decides to fold, he loses the £1 that he has already staked.

Look at Figure 3.1a–c.

Player 1 is the dealer, as indicated by the dealer button. Player 2 makes the small blind bet and player 3 makes the big blind bet. After the pocket cards have been dealt, the first person to act is player 4. The arrows show the direction in which action is taken around the table.

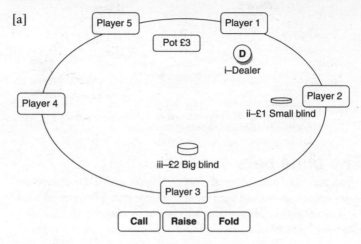

[a]

In the first betting round, if no one has raised the big blind, the player in the big blind position may check or raise.

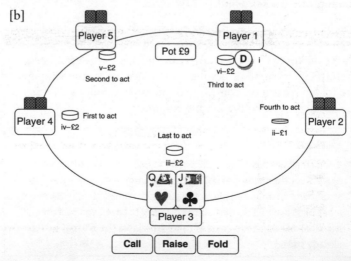

[b]

Now there are just three players left: players 1, 2 and 3. Each of these players has so far contributed £4 to the pot. Players 4 and 5 have each contributed £2 to the pot. As players 4 and 5 have folded, they have lost what they put into the pot. The game then continues to the flop.

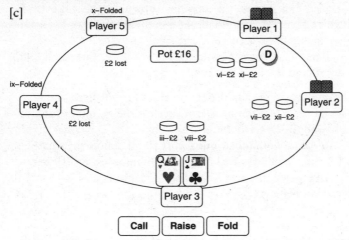

Figure 3.1 Blind bets

The following table shows a summary of the betting that has taken place:

Player	Action taken	Pot (£)	Figure	Number	Notes
1	Dealer	0	3.2a	i	
2	Small blind £1	1		ii	
3	Big blind £1	3		iii	
4	Calls £2	5	3.2b	iv	
5	Calls £2	7		v	
1	Calls £2	9		vi	
2	Calls £1	10	3.2c	vii	£1 has already been bet as the small blind
3	Raises £2	12		viii	
4	Folds	12		ix	
5	Folds	12		x	
1	Calls £2	14		xi	
2	Calls £2	16		xii	

Type of game and betting minimums

When you see a game advertised it will show two amounts and an abbreviation for the type of game. For example: £1/£2 FL; £5/£10 NL; £2/£4 PL.

For fixed-limit games, the amounts shown are the stakes of the small and big bet. The small blind is equal to half of the small bet. The big blind is equal to the small bet. For a £1/£2 FL game, the small bet is £1 and the big bet is £2. The small blind is £0.50 and the big blind is £1.

The amounts represent different values for pot-limit and no-limit games. Here the smaller number is the amount of the small blind and the larger number is the big blind. The larger number is also the minimum bet. For a £5/£10 NL game, the small blind is £5, the big blind is £10 and the minimum bet is £10. For a £2/£4 PL game, the small blind is £2, the big blind is £4 and the minimum bet is £4.

Remember this: The number of chips needed

The number of chips needed to play a game depends on the type of betting system and how tightly you play. Fixed-limit games require the least amount of chips. As a general guide you should start with 300 times the big bet. If the big bet is £2 then you will need at least £600 in chips. Pot-limit and no-limit require considerably more at around 1,000 to 2,000 times the big blind.

Fixed-limit games

Fixed-limit poker is abbreviated to FL. With fixed-limit games you will know in advance roughly how much it will cost you to play. Because there is a limit on how much can be bet, players tend to stay in the game for longer. This means that with this form of betting the games tend to end in more showdowns than pot-limit and no-limit.

When you see a game of fixed-limit poker advertised, it will show the stakes as two numbers, for example £2/4 or £5/10. The first number is the amount of the small bet and equal to the big blind, with the second number representing the big bet. In a £2/4 game the small blind is £1 and the big blind £2. The small bet is £2 and the big bet £4.

In the first two rounds of betting, the bets and raises will be £2 and in the third and fourth rounds the bets and raises will be £4.

In some games unlimited raises may be allowed when there are just two players left. It is therefore vitally important that you check the rules before playing; otherwise, a game could cost you much more than you anticipated.

Fixed-limit games consist of small bets and big bets. The bets and raises during the first two betting rounds (pre-flop and flop) are equal to the big blind and are called the small bet. The next two bets and raises are equal to twice the big blind and are called the big bet. In most games the number of raises is limited to three per betting round. The maximum number of bets that a player can make during each betting round is four.

These bets consist of:

1 bet

2 raise

3 re-raise

4 cap.

WHAT IS THE MAXIMUM IT COSTS TO PLAY?

In a £2/£4 FL game, before the cards are dealt it will cost you nothing, £1 or £2 depending on whether or not you have to make one of the blind bets. If you make the small blind and fold, the game would have cost you £1. If you make the big blind and fold, the game would have cost you £2. If you need to participate in every betting round for the maximum number of bets, the game will cost you 12 times the big bet – in this example 12 × 4 = £48.

Blind bet 0, small blind £1, big blind £2

Pocket cards

Round 1   4 × small bet = £8

Flop

Round 2   4 × small bet = £8

River

Round 3   4 × big bet = £16

Turn

Round 4   4 × big bet = £16

Total = £48

The maximum cost of the game will be £48.

Let's look at this in action. Suppose there are five players – a, b, c, d and e – in a £1/2 FL game:

▶ Player a is the dealer.

▶ Player b makes the small blind bet £0.50.

▶ Player c makes the big blind bet £1.

The pocket cards are dealt.

▶ Player d is the first to act. He has the option to fold, bet or raise. To continue in the game he must place a bet at least equal to the big blind – £1. If he wants to raise, then he must place a bet of £2. This is £1 to match the big blind plus a raise of £1.

▶ Player d chooses to raise. He contributes £2 to the pot.

▶ Player a is the next to act. In order to stay in the game, his bet must equal that of player d. He also chooses to raise. He raises by £1. His total bet consists of the stake to call player d's bet plus the amount of the raise. His total stake is £3 (£2 to match the bet and £1 to raise).

- Player b is the next to act. In order to stay in the game, his bet must equal that of player a. Player a's total stake is £3. Player b has already bet £0.50 as the small blind. So, to match player a's bet, he needs to bet another £2.50. This makes his total contribution to the pot so far £3. He does this.

- Player c is the next to act. He needs to make a bet that is equal to that of player b. Player c has already made a bet of £1 with the big blind so needs to bet £2 to make his contribution to the pot £3. He does this.

- Player d is next to act. The stakes have been raised to £3. As he has only contributed £2 so far, he needs to add another £1 to call player c's stakes. He decides to raise another £1. His bet this time is £2 (£1 to match the bet and £1 to raise), bringing his total stakes to £4.

This is the third and final raise in this betting round. If the other players want to continue in the game, they need to match the £4 total stakes.

- Player a has so far contributed £3. He decides to fold. He takes no further part in the game and loses the £3 that he has already bet.

- Player b decides to call and bets another £1. He has now made a total bet of £4 that matches player d's bet.

- Player c also decides to call and bets another £1. He has now made a total bet of £4 that matches player d's bet.

All of the money bet now goes into the pot. This is £3 from player a, £4 from player b, £4 from player c and £4 from player d. The total pot is £15. This betting round is now over. The remaining players have all contributed the same amount of money to the pot. Player a's contribution is smaller as he decided to fold.

The flop is dealt. Players b, c and d now compete in the next betting round. The betting limits for this round are the same as the first: £1 to bet and £1 to raise.

- Player b is the first to act in this round of betting as he is located to the left of the dealer. Player b makes a bet of £1.

- Player c raises – his bet is £1 to match b's bet and £1 for the raise, giving a total stake of £2.

- Player d folds. He takes no further part in the game.

- Player b calls player c's rise by making a bet of £1.

Both players have now contributed the same amount in the betting round. This money is added to the pot. Player b bet £2, player c bet £2, and player d folded. The total pot is now £19.

The turn is dealt. Only player b and player c are left to compete in the next round of betting. The limits for the betting round are increased to £2 for a bet and £2 for a raise.

- Player b goes first. He bets £2.

- Player c raises (his bet is £2 to match b's bet and £2 to raise). His stakes are £4.

- Player b calls £2. This matches player c's bet of £4.

This betting round ends. Both players have bet an additional £4, giving a total of £8. This is added to the pot. The pot is now £27.

The river is dealt.

- Player b bets £2.

- Player c raises (£2 to match b's bet plus £2 to raise) . Bet = £4

- Player b raises a further £2 (£2 to match c's bet and £2 to raise). Bet = £4

- Player c calls £2.

Both players have now contributed a further £6 each to the pot. The pot is now £39.

A showdown now takes place. The player with the highest-ranking hand wins.

The following table shows a summary of the betting that has taken place:

Stage	Player	Action	Amount bet per round (£)	Added to pot (£)	Pot total (£)
Pre-flop	a	Dealer			
	b	Small blind	0.50	0.50	0.50
	c	Big blind	1	1	1.50
	d	Raises £1	2	2	3.50
	a	Raises £1	3	3	6.50
	b	Calls £2.50	3	2.50	9
	c	Calls £2	3	2	11
	d	Raises £1	4	2	13
	a	Folds	3	0	13
	b	Calls £1	4	1	14
	c	Calls £1	4	1	15
The flop	b	Bets £1	1	1	16
	c	Raises £1	2	2	18
	d	Folds	0	0	18
	b	Calls £1	2	1	19
The turn	b	Bets £2	2	2	21
	c	Raises £2	4	4	25
	b	Calls £2	4	2	27
The river	b	Bets £2	2	2	29
	c	Raises £2	4	4	33
	b	Raises £2	6	4	37
	c	Calls £2	6	2	39

Pot-limit games

A pot-limit game allows the player to make a raise anywhere in between the minimum specified for the game up to a maximum of the amount that is in the pot after the call has been made.

To calculate the maximum allowed raise, the total amount of money in the pot is added to the amount needed to call the previous bet.

Example

If there is £3 in the pot and you need to bet £2 to call, you are then able to make a maximum raise of the amount in the pot plus the amount of the call.

Maximum raise = 3 + 2 = £5.

Total stake = the amount to call + the amount of the raise = 2 + 5 = 7.

You add £7 to the pot. The total in the pot is now £10.

The following player must then fold or match your bet. To call the bet they need to add £7 to the pot. This matches your bet. This creates a new pot of £17. They decide to raise the maximum amount. The raise is the value of the new pot, which is £17. The total bet made is the £17 raise plus the £7 call = £24.

If you want to easily calculate the maximum raise, it is two times the call plus the current pot. For example, if there is £100 in the pot and you need to bet £10 to call, the maximum raise is (10 × 2) + £100 = £120.

Here are two further examples in table form:

EXAMPLE 1

Player	Action	Total bet (£)	Calculation	Pot (£)
1	Small blind £1	1		1
2	Big blind £2	2		3
3	Raises maximum £5	7	2 + 2 + 3	10
4	Raises maximum £17	24	7 + 7 + 10	34

EXAMPLE 2

Player	Action	Total bet (£)	Calculation	Pot (£)
				10
1	Bets £10	10	10	20
2	Raises maximum £30	40	10 + 10 + 20	60
3	Raises maximum £100	140	40 + 40 + 60	200
1	Calls £130	130	140 − 10	330
2	Calls £100	100	140 − 40	430

Often bets are required to be made in multiples of a stake unit. For example: bets may be required to be made in multiples of £5 or £10 in order to make calculations easier. Where the multiple is £5 a raise of £25 would be allowed (5 × 5) but not £28.

No-limit games

No-limit games have a minimum bet and a maximum bet that is limited to the number of chips that a player has on the table. A player may bet all of his chips. The games are played with a fixed small and big blind. In a £10/20 NL game, the small blind is £10, the big blind is £20 and the minimum bet is £20. The amount that you can bet will be limited by how many chips your opponents have. If, for example, you have a stack of £5,000 and you are up against one player who has just £2,000 left, the maximum that you can win against this player is £2,000. As soon as this player has put all his chips in the pot, you have reached the maximum bet.

If, however, there are two other players left, and player 1 has £2,000, player 2 has £20,000 and you have £5,000, the most that you can win from player 1 is £2,000 and the most that you can win from player 2 is £5,000 (the amount equal to your stack).

When you have put all of your chips in the pot, you have reached the maximum bet. Betting all of your chips is called all-in.

Pocket cards

Player a	Player b	Player c
A♠ Q♥	K♦ K♣	Q♦ K♠

The flop
Q♣ K♥ Q♠

The turn
Q♣ K♥ Q♠ 5♦

The river
Q♣ K♥ Q♠ 5♦ 2♠

Player a's hand
Q♥ Q♣ Q♠ A♠ K♥

Player b's hand
K♦ K♣ K♥ Q♣ Q♠

Player c's hand
Q♦ Q♣ Q♠ K♠ K♥

The following table shows the betting for a £5/10 NL:

Round	Player	Action	Pot 1	Pot 2	Notes
Binds	a	Dealer			
	b	Small blind £5	5		
	c	Big blind £10	15		
Pre-flop	a	Raises £50	75		Call 10 + raise 50 = 60
	b	Calls £55	130		60 – 5 small blind
	c	Calls £50	180		60 – 10 small blind
Flop	b	Goes all-in £220	400		Bets all his chips
	c	Calls £220	620		
	a	Raises £800	840	800	220 goes in pot 1 to call b's bet. The 800 raise goes into a second pot.
	c	Calls a's raise		1,600	
Turn	c	Goes all-in £500		2,100	
	a	Calls £500		2,600	

Player b goes all-in and contributes to the pot up until the second round of betting. A second pot is then started. All subsequent bets are placed into the second pot. The players continue the game. At the turn, player c has gone all-in. The final card is dealt. There is no more betting as player c has run out of chips. The showdown now takes place. All the players' hands are compared in the showdown for the first pot. Player b has a full house (three kings and two queens) and so wins the first pot of £840.

Player a's and player c's hands are compared in the showdown for the second pot. Player a has three of a kind (three queens) and player c has a full house (queens over kings). Player c wins the second pot of £2,600.

Although player b has a higher hand than player c, he cannot compete for the second pot as he has contributed no money to it.

Test your knowledge (answers at the back)

1   In a £1/£2 FL game: a) How much is the small blind? b) How much is the big blind?

2   In a £5/£10 FL game: a) How much is the small blind? b) How much is the big blind?

3   In a £50/£100 NL game: a) How much is the small blind? b) How much is the big blind?

4   In a £2/£4 NL game: a) How much is the small blind? b) How much is the big blind?

5   In a £10/£20 PL game: a) How much is the small blind? b) How much is the big blind?

6   In a £1/£2 PL game: a) How much is the small blind? b) How much is the big blind?

7   What is the minimum bet after the flop in a £10/£20 FL game?

8   What is the minimum raise after the flop in a £5/£10 FL game?

9   What is the minimum bet after the turn in a £1/£2 FL game?

10 What is the maximum raise after the river in a £50/£100 FL game?

11 Player 3 is the dealer: who makes the small blind and who makes the big blind?

12 Player 6 is the dealer: who makes the small blind and who makes the big blind?

13 Player 4 has made a bet of £10: can player 5 check?

14 Player 1 has made the small blind of £5. Player 2 has made the big blind. Player 3 has called £10. The other players have folded. How much must player 1 bet to stay in the game?

15 In a pot-limit game, the pot is £100. You need to call £20. What is the maximum raise and how much in total would you need to contribute to the pot?

16 In a pot-limit game, the pot is £250. You need to call £40. What is the maximum raise and how much in total would you need to contribute to the pot?

17 In a pot-limit game, the pot is £200. The previous player called £50. What is the maximum raise and how much in total would you need to contribute to the pot?

18 What is the minimum bet in a 20/40 NL game?

19 At the start of the game, player a has £500, player b has £1,000 and you have £200 in chips. What is the maximum that you could win if all players stay to the showdown?

20 Player a has gone all-in at the flop. He has the highest hand in the showdown. The first pot contains £250. The second pot contains £600. How much does player a win?

Next step

You should now have an understanding of how the betting is organized for the different games of hold 'em. You should be able to calculate how much to add to the pot. The next chapter explains how to calculate the odds of hold 'em. It will help you to decide whether or not staying in the game or folding is the best move.

4

The odds

In this chapter you will learn:

▶ *What odds are*
▶ *The odds of making a ranking hand*
▶ *The odds of improving a hand at the flop/turn*
▶ *The odds of improving a hand at the river*
▶ *How to easily calculate the odds*
▶ *Detailed calculations of the odds*
▶ *Pot odds.*

What are odds?

In order to play poker well, a sound understanding of the odds of being dealt particular hands is essential. You may have played other games of poker such as five-card draw or seven-card stud. You need to bear in mind that Texas hold 'em is different and as such needs a different strategy. What may have been a good hand in other forms of poker will not necessarily be so good when playing hold 'em.

With a thorough understanding of the odds, you can decide whether your hand is worth playing or should be folded. Throughout the game of Texas hold 'em the odds of achieving a particular hand change depending on what cards you have been dealt. At each stage of the game you have a chance of improving on your hand with the next round of cards being dealt. You need to know the chances of improving your hand. You also need to know what the chances are of the other players having a hand that beats yours. It is also important to consider how much money is in the pot and whether or not you are betting at the right level.

There are a number of methods available to help you calculate the odds. Of course, you can calculate the odds yourself if your maths skills are fast enough. Alternatively, you can use charts, software or apps to calculate the odds for you. The more quickly you can find the odds the better, so that you can take the appropriate action within the time limit imposed. As a beginner, you will find it easier to use a chart or software for the calculations. With experience, you will be able to memorize your chances of making particular hands and learn what is the most appropriate move – betting, raising, bluffing or folding.

How to calculate the odds

Odds consist of two numbers: for example 12/1, 2/1, 3/1. They express the chances of making an outcome against the chances of not making an outcome. With odds of 12/1 there is 1 chance of making the outcome for every 12 chances there are of not making the outcome.

You will often see chances of making hands in poker expressed in percentages. These are the number of chances of getting the outcome in one hundred chances. It will be down to personal choice how you prefer to calculate the odds.

Remember this: Calculating percentages from odds

For calculating percentages from odds the following formula is used:

$$\frac{100}{A+B} = percentage$$

where A = the chances against and B = the chances for.

Thus, if the odds are 4/1 against, then the percentage odds will be:

$$\frac{100}{4+1} = 20 \text{ per cent}$$

Remember this: Calculating odds from percentages

For calculating percentages from odds the following formula is used:

$$\frac{100}{A} - 1 = odds/1$$

where A = the percentage odds.

Thus, if the percentage is 20, then the odds will be:

$$\frac{100}{20} - 1 = 5 - 1 = 4/1$$

A pack of cards consists of 52 cards. Your chances of getting an ace dealt as your first card are 4 out of 52 as there are four aces in a pack. Four cards will give you an ace while 48 cards will not. Expressed as odds, this is 48/4 or 12/1. Suppose you are dealt the ace with your first card, the chances of the second ace being dealt are now reduced because there are only three aces left in the pack while there are 48 other cards left. The odds are now 48/3, or 16/1, against.

To find your chances of getting dealt a diamond with your first card, you need to consider that there are 13 diamonds in the pack and 39 other cards. The odds are 39/13, or 3/1. If your first card is a diamond, the odds of being dealt a diamond as your second card are calculated as follows. There are now 12 diamonds left in the deck and 39 other cards. The odds are now 39/12 or 3.25/1 against being dealt a second diamond.

Throughout the game of poker you will want to know what your odds are of making a particular hand at different stages of the game. This will help you to decide whether your hand is worth playing or should be folded.

Example

Suppose your pocket cards are two spades and the flop contains two spades. You are now holding four spades for a possible flush.

   Pocket cards: As, 7s

   Flop: 6s, Qs, 9d

To calculate your chances of making your flush on the turn, you need to consider how many spades are left in the deck and how many other cards there are. There are 13 spades in total. You know that four have already been dealt so there are nine left. There are 52 cards in total, of which the five above have been dealt, leaving 47 cards. Nine could be spades, which leaves 38 other cards. The odds of getting a spade on the next card are therefore 38/9, or 4.2/1.

As a percentage this is:

$$\frac{100}{4.22 + 1} = 19.16 \text{ per cent}$$

If you fail to get a spade on the turn, you can then calculate the odds of getting it on the river. There are still nine spades in the deck and, because one more card has been dealt, there are now 37 other cards. The odds of getting a spade on the river are now 37/9, or 4.1/1.

As a percentage this is:

$$\frac{100}{4.11 + 1} = 19.56 \text{ per cent}$$

In this same example another player may have pocket queens, which means that on the flop he has three of kind with queens. The odds of achieving four of a kind with queens on the turn are calculated as follows.

There is only one queen left in the deck. Five cards have been dealt so far. There are 52 − 5 = 47 left. There are therefore one queen and 46 other cards. The odds of getting the queen are 46/1.

As a percentage this is:

$$\frac{100}{46+1} = 2.12 \text{ per cent}$$

There is a greater chance that the player will make the flush than that the player will make the four of a kind with queens.

How the odds change with Texas hold 'em

In poker, 52 cards are used to make five-card hands. When five-card hands are dealt there are 2,649,920 different possible hands that can be dealt:

$$\frac{52 \times 52 \times 50 \times 49 \times 48}{1 \times 2 \times 3 \times 4 \times 5} = 2,649,920$$

The following table shows the odds against being dealt a particular hand by the flop:

Hand	Number of ways hand can be made	Odds against being dealt by the flop
Royal flush	4	649,739/1
Straight flush	36	72,192/1
Four of a kind	624	4,164/1
Full house	3,744	693/1
Flush	5,108	508/1
Straight	10,200	254/1
Three of a kind	54,912	46/1
Two pair	123,552	20/1
One pair	1,098,240	15/1
Highest card	1,302,540	1/1

You may be familiar with the fact that often a pair is enough to win games like draw poker. However, with Texas hold 'em the chances of getting a pair are vastly increased. The odds shown in the table above show you the chances of making a hand at the flop – that is, when five cards have been dealt.

In Texas hold 'em you have a choice of seven cards with which to make a hand. The final two cards that are dealt to the hand drastically change the odds of being dealt a ranking hand.

To appreciate just how rare the higher-ranking hands are when only five cards are dealt, consider how long it takes to play 649,740 hands. If you play, for example, an average of one hand every five minutes, you would need to continue playing constantly for approximately six years and two months. Playing for a few hours each week, you can see that the chances of being dealt a royal flush at the flop are very rare.

Try it now: The low chances of being dealt a higher-ranking hand

Take a pack of cards and deal them out into five-card poker hands. By continually repeating this you will begin to appreciate just how rare it is to be dealt one of the higher-ranking hands by the flop. You will also start to get some idea about which hands are worth playing.

If poker is played with only five cards and no further cards are dealt from the pack, players are mostly competing with low-ranking hands. By increasing the number of cards dealt, the chances of having a higher-ranking hand are increased.

In Texas hold 'em, a five-card poker hand is made from seven cards. With seven cards you are able to make up 21 different five-card poker hands. This is the reason that higher-ranking hands are more common in hold 'em.

$$\frac{7 \times 6 \times 5 \times 4 \times 3}{1 \times 2 \times 3 \times 4 \times 5} = 21$$

In a game of Texas hold 'em there are 133,784,560 possible combinations of seven cards compared with 2,649,920 combinations of five cards. In Texas hold 'em the number of combinations increases fivefold:

$$\frac{52 \times 51 \times 50 \times 49 \times 48 \times 47 \times 46}{1 \times 2 \times 3 \times 4 \times 5 \times 6 \times 7} = 133,784,560$$

This hugely improves each player's chances of achieving a higher-ranking hand. By looking at the cards that each player is showing, or the community cards, you can deduce the possible hand that they may hold and calculate the chances of them having that particular hand.

The following table shows the number of ways that a Texas hold 'em hand can be made:

Royal flush	4,324
Straight flush	37,260
Four of a kind	224,848
Full house	3,473,184
Flush	4,047,644
Straight	6,180,020
Three of a kind	6,461,620
Two pair	31,433,400
One pair	58,627,800
Highest card	23,294,460
Total	133,784,560

Calculating the number of hands

There are four ways in which a royal flush can be made when five cards are dealt:

1 As, Ks, Qs, Js, 10s

2 Ah, Kh, Qh, Jh, 10h

3 Ac, Kc, Qc, Jc, 10c

4 Ad, Kd, Qd, Jd, 10d

With Texas hold 'em an extra two cards are dealt. After the initial five cards there are now 47 left in the pack: 52 – 5 = 47.

The remaining 47 cards can be dealt $\frac{47 \times 46}{1 \times 2}$ ways = 1,081.

The total number of ways that a royal flush can be made = 4 × 1,081 = 4,324.

There are 133,784,560 hands divided by 4,324, which gives 30,940 chances of making a royal flush, or odds of 30,939/1.

So with five cards the odds are 649,739/1 and with seven cards the odds of making a royal flush are 30,939/1. This means there is 21 times the chance of making a royal flush with seven cards as there is with five cards.

Calculating the odds for the pocket cards

The first two cards you receive are the pocket cards. Your first decision is to fold or play with the pocket cards. You need to decide whether the pocket cards are good or bad. In the table below you can see that the odds against receiving particular pocket cards vary greatly. The highest pocket card combination is AK suited, with odds against being dealt it of 331/1. These pocket cards open the possibility of a royal flush. A pair of aces has odds against of 220/1. With ten players, one in 22 games has the possibility of a pair of aces being dealt as pocket cards.

The following table shows the odds against getting particular pocket cards:

AK suited	331/1
AA	220/1
KK	220/1
QQ	220/1
AK	110/1
Any pair	16/1
Two cards J or higher	10/1
A	5.25/1
Any pair or ace	3.9/1
Two cards suited	3.25/1

THE ODDS OF GETTING POCKET ACES

There are four aces in a deck, which can be dealt in six different ways to make a pair of aces. The following figure shows the ways in which a pair of aces can be dealt.

▶ Method 1

Step 1: Calculating the number of ways an ace can be dealt as a pair:

$$\frac{4 \times 3}{1 \times 2} = 6$$

Step 2: Calculating the number of ways a two-card hand can be dealt. From 52 cards, 1,326 two-card hands can be dealt:

$$\frac{52 \times 51}{1 \times 2} = 1,326$$

Dividing step 2 by step 1:

$$\frac{1,326}{6} = 221$$

The odds against getting pocket aces are therefore 220/1.

▶ Method 2

An alternative method for calculating this is to consider that there are four aces in the pack of 52 cards. There are four chances of being dealt an ace from 52 cards with the first card and then three chances of being dealt the second from the remaining 51 cards.

$$\frac{52 \times 51}{4 \times 3} = 13 \times 17 = 221,$$

or odds of 220/1 against being dealt two aces as pocket cards.

THE ODDS AGAINST GETTING ANY PAIR

There are 13 possible pairs and each pair can be dealt six ways:

$$\frac{1,326}{(13 \times 6)} = 17$$

The odds against getting any pair are 16/1.

CALCULATING THE ODDS OF IMPROVING FROM A PAIR TO THREE OF A KIND ON THE FLOP

Suppose your two pocket cards are aces. You want to know the odds of getting a third ace on the flop.

There are 50 cards left in the deck. These can be dealt the following number of ways:

$$\frac{50 \times 49 \times 48}{3 \times 2 \times 1} = 19,600$$

There are two cards that could be used to make the three of a kind. That leaves 48 other cards in the deck. They can be dealt the following number of ways:

$$\frac{48 \times 47 \times 46}{3 \times 2 \times 1} = 17,296$$

The number of three-card combinations that could contain one ace is:

$$19,600 - 17,296 = 2,304$$

$$17,296/2,304 = 7.5/1$$

Therefore, the odds are 7.5/1 against getting another ace in the flop.

Calculating the odds of improving on your hand

To work out your chances of improving your hand, you need to consider how many cards are in the pack, how many you have been dealt so far and how many cards could complete your hand.

The number of cards that could complete your hand to particular ranking hands are called outs. Depending on what cards you have been dealt so far, you will have different numbers of outs. Some outs will be more useful to you than others. Knowing the number of outs tells you how easy or difficult it is going to be to improve your hand to a higher-ranking hand. With a large number of outs you have a greater chance of improving your hand. With a low number of outs you have a lower chance of improving your hand and it will be more difficult to reach the desired hand.

It is important to bear in mind the make-up of a pack of cards to work out your odds of improving a hand. A pack consists of 52 cards. For each number there are four cards – four aces, four queens, four 10s, etc. If, for example, you have two cards of the same number for a pair, there are only two other cards that can make a three of a kind or four of a kind.

For each suit there are 13 cards – that is, 13 hearts, 13 diamonds, 13 spades and 13 clubs. For example: Ah, Kh, Qh, Jh, 10h, 9h, 8h, 7h, 6h, 5h, 4h, 3h, 2h. If you have three cards to a flush, there are ten other cards that could complete the flush. If you have four cards to a flush, then there are nine other cards that could complete the flush.

Often, there will be several better hands that could be made after the flop. Four cards to a flush may be improved to a straight flush, a flush or a straight. Depending on which cards you have missing, there could be several cards that will be helpful to complete a good-ranking hand.

Once you know how many outs you have, you can then calculate the odds of achieving that hand. Knowing the odds will then help you to decide whether or not to continue playing or to fold. Knowing the odds will also help you to calculate how much to bet. You are able to compare how much is in the pot with how much it will cost you to win that amount. This is explained in greater detail in the pot odds section later in the chapter.

Although cards have been dealt to the other players, because you do not know what these cards are you still have to include them in the calculations to get an accurate idea of the odds. You can only base your calculation on the cards you can see in your hand and those exposed in the community cards.

Counting the outs

Depending on what pocket cards you have and what you get in the flop, you can work out what cards you need to make your desired hand. Examples for certain situations are given below. Some cards can be used to complete more than one desired hand, but it is important to count that card only once.

For example: you may need the ace of diamonds to complete a flush or it may also be useful to complete a straight. Although the card is useful twice, it can only be counted as one out. You can also apply these calculations to the theoretical hands that your opponents may be holding.

ONE HIGH CARD TO A HIGH PAIR

Pocket cards: As, 4d

Flop: 7h, Jd, 8c

To make a pair of aces you need Ac, Ah or Ad. A total of three cards could give this hand. There are therefore three outs.

ONE CARD TO A PAIR OR HIGHER

Pocket cards: Kd, Qs

Flop: 8d, 4s, 10c

To make a pair of kings or a pair of queens you need Kc, Ks, Kh or Qd, Qc, Qh – six cards in total. Two or more of these cards would also give you three of a kind, a full house or four of a kind. There are six outs.

INSIDE STRAIGHT

Pocket cards: Kd, Qc

Flop: 10h, 9s, 2c

To complete the straight any jack is needed: Js, Jc, Jh, Jd – four cards in total. There are four outs.

TWO PAIR TO FULL HOUSE

Pocket cards: Ad, Jh

Flop: Js, Ac, 9d

Here the hand is currently two pair: Ad, Ac, Jh, Js, 9d. To improve to a full house, another ace or another jack is needed: Ah, As, Jc or Jd – four cards in total. There are four outs.

ONE PAIR TO TWO PAIR, SET, FULL HOUSE OR FOUR OF A KIND

Pocket cards: Qc, Ks

Flop: Qd, 10h, 7s

The hand is currently one pair: Qc, Qd, Ks, 10h, 7s. To improve to three of a kind with queens, a further queen is required. To improve to four of a kind, both queens are needed. For two pair, another king is needed. Another 10 or another 7 would also give two pair. A pair of 10s or a pair of 7s would give a full house. So any of the following cards would give an improvement: Qh, Qs, Kh, Kd, Kc, 10s, 10d, 10c, 7h, 7d, 7s – 11 cards in total. There are therefore 11 outs.

THREE OF A KIND TO FULL HOUSE OR FOUR OF A KIND

Pocket cards: Js, Jh

Flop: Jd, 10d, 3h

The hand is currently three of a kind with jacks: Js, Jh, Jd, 10d, 3h. It could improve to a full house or four of a kind with jacks. To make the four of a kind, the last jack is needed – Jc. For this, there is just one out. To make a full house another 10 or another 3 is needed. The following cards would give this possibility: 10s, 10h, 10c or 3s, 3d, 3c. There are six outs to make that hand. In addition, a full house could be made by any pair of cards – any two of A, K, Q, 9, 8, 7, 6, 5, 4, 2. There are four of each of these cards: $4 \times 10 = 40$. In total, there are $1 + 6 + 40 = 47$ outs.

▶ After the turn

Pocket cards: Js, Jh

Community cards: Jd, 10d, 3h, Ac

Here the turn has been dealt. The hand is still three of a kind with jacks: Js, Jh, Jd, Ac, 10d. The fourth jack was not dealt; neither was a card to make the full house. The number of outs can be recalculated. The fourth jack is still needed to make four of a kind – Jc, or one out. To make the full house, another ace, 10 or 3 is needed. The following cards are useful: Jc, As, Ah, Ad, 10s, 10h, 10c, 3s, 3d, 3c. This is ten cards in total. The number of outs has now been reduced to ten.

OPEN STRAIGHT

Pocket cards: Kd, Qd

Flop: Jh, 10c, 5s

The hand is currently Kd, Qd, Jh, 10c, 5s. To improve to a straight, either an ace or a 9 is needed: As, Ah, Ad, Ac or 9s, 9h, 9d, 9c. To complete the straight, there are eight outs.

To make three of a kind, another king or another queen is needed: Ks, Kh, Kc, Qs, Qh, Qc. To complete the three of a kind, there are six outs. To make a high two pair with kings or queens, another king or queen is also needed. In total, to make a decent-ranking hand there are 14 outs.

FLUSH

Pocket cards: As, 8s

Flop: Kh, 4s, 2s

The hand is currently four cards to a flush (four spades): As, 8s, 4s, 2s, Kh. To complete the flush, any of the other spades is needed: Ks, Qs, Js, 10s, 9s, 7s, 6s, 5s, 3s. There are nine outs.

FLUSH AND INSIDE STRAIGHT

Pocket cards: Kd, Qd

Flop: Jd, 9d, 3h

The hand is currently four cards to a flush (four diamonds). The 10d will give a straight flush and any of the other diamonds will complete the flush. In addition, any of the other 10s will give a straight.

The cards that will be useful are Ad, 10d, 8d, 7d, 6d, 5d, 4d, 3d, 2d and 10h, 10c, 10s. There are therefore 12 outs.

FLUSH AND OPEN STRAIGHT

Pocket cards: Qc, Jc

Flop: Kc, 10c, 4s

The hand is currently four cards to a flush (four clubs) and open straight (the straight can be completed at either end): Kc, Qc, Jc, 10c, 4s. To complete a straight flush, Ac or 9c is needed. To make a flush, any of the other clubs is needed. In addition, any ace or any nine will complete the straight. The cards that will be useful are Ac, 9c, 8c, 7c, 6c, 5c, 4c, 3c, 2c, Ah, As, Ad, 9s, 9h, 9d. There are a total of 15 useful cards. There are 15 outs.

▶ **At the turn**

  Pocket cards: Qc, Jc

  Community cards: Kc, 10c, 4s, 9d

The hand is now a straight Kc, Qc, Jc, 10c, 9d. It could still be improved to a straight flush with the Ac or 9c, to a flush with any of the other clubs, or to a higher straight with any of the aces. The cards that could be useful are Ac, 9c, 8c, 7c, 6c, 5c, 4c, 3c, 2c, As, Ad, Ah. There are 12 cards that could be useful. There are thus 12 outs that could further improve the hand.

An easy way to calculate percentage chances of making a hand

Once you know the number of outs, you can calculate your percentage chances of making the hand. An easy way to calculate the approximate percentage chances of getting a hand at the turn or at the river is to multiply the number of outs by two. This does not give you the exact number, but is a much quicker calculation to make while playing than the more complex accurate calculation.

For example:

▶ If there are 11 outs: 11 × 2 = 22-per-cent chance of making the hand

▶ If there are 17 outs: 17 × 2 = 34-per-cent chance of making the hand

▶ If there are 4 outs: 4 × 2 = 8-per-cent chance of making the hand.

Accurately calculating the chances of improving a hand

This method of calculating is more complex but gives the accurate odds of improving. You need to know how many outs there are and how many other cards are left in the deck. After the turn, you can recalculate the odds based on what card is dealt on the turn. This card may or may not have helped your hand. Even if it did not and you have the same number of outs, the chances of making the hand will be slightly less because on the river there is always one less card in the deck as it has been dealt on the turn.

EXAMPLE 1

Pocket cards: Ks, Kd

Flop: Qd, 8s, 6h

Here, after the pocket cards have been dealt, you have two kings. The flop has failed to improve the hand. To improve to a three of a kind you need another king; to improve to four of a kind you need two kings. To improve to a full house, you need another king with another queen, 8 or 6. Alternatively, you need either two queens, two 8s or two 6s. Another queen, 8 or 6 would also give you two pair.

To improve to any of these hands, you have the following cards still in the deck – two kings, three queens, three 8s and three 6s. This gives you a total of 2 + 3 + 3 + 3 = 11 cards that would improve your hand. The odds of an improvement on the next card are 36/11, or 3.27/1. As a percentage this is 100/4.27 = 23.41 per cent.

▶ **After the turn**

Pocket cards: Ks, Kd

Community cards: Qd, 8s, 6h, Kh

At the turn, a third king has been dealt. This now gives the opportunity of improving to four of a kind with kings or a full house with another queen, 8 or 6. The cards that would be useful are Kc, Qs, Qh, Qc, 8h, 8d, 8c, 6s, 6d, 6c – in total, ten cards, or ten outs.

You can also see that there is a danger that another player could have pocket queens, giving a current hand of three of a kind with queens. This player has just one out that could complete that hand. If you deduct the queens from your outs, you still have seven outs compared to just one out for the other player.

There is also a possible straight if a player has pocket J, 10 cards. This player needs an ace or a 9. He has eight outs.

There is also the possibility of a flush. A player may have pocket hearts, giving him four hearts to a flush. Since there are 13 hearts, this player has nine outs.

There is also the possibility that a player has pocket aces. He has only two outs to give him a better three of a kind than you currently have.

With this analysis, you can see that you have the most outs and are therefore in the best position.

EXAMPLE 2

> *Pocket cards:* Qd, Jd
>
> *Flop:* 9d, 10s, As

At the flop there are:

▶ three cards to a flush: Qd, Jd, 9d

▶ three cards to a straight ace high: As, Qd, Jd, 10s.

▶ four cards to a straight Qd, Jd, 10s, 9d.

So:

▶ To complete the flush, two more diamonds are needed. There are ten diamonds left in the deck. Total outs = 10.

▶ To complete the ace high straight, a king is needed. The Kd has been counted above, so there are another three outs.

▶ To complete the four-card straight, a king or an 8 is needed. The kings have been counted above. With the 8s there are another four outs.

In total, there are 17 outs.

The chances of getting one of the cards on the turn is 30/17, or 1.76/1. That is a 36-per-cent chance.

EXAMPLE 3

> *Pocket cards:* Ad, Ks
>
> *Flop:* Jh, 3h, 10c

The hand at this stage is an incomplete straight Ad, Ks, Jh, 10c, 3h. A queen is needed to complete the straight. There are four queens in the deck. This gives four outs. There are 52 – 5 = 47 cards left in the deck. Four are queens and 47 – 4 = 43 other cards. The odds of getting the queen on the turn are 43/4, or

10.75/1. If the queen does not appear on the turn, the odds of getting it on the river are 42/4, or 10.5/1.

EXAMPLE 4

Pocket cards: Ks, Qd

Flop: Kd, 7s, Qh

Here the hand is currently two pair: Ks, Kd, Qd, Qh, 7s. To achieve a full house, either another king or another queen is needed. To achieve four of a kind with kings or queens, either another two kings or another two queens are needed. There are four kings and four queens in a pack of cards. Two of each have already been dealt. This leaves two kings and two queens in the deck. There are therefore four outs. There are 47 − 4 = 43 other cards. The odds of getting either a king or queen on the turn are 43/4, or 10.75/1.

The following table shows the outs and chances of making the hand:

	Chances of making the desired hand			
	On the turn		On the river	
Number of outs	*Odds*	*Percentage*	*Odds*	*Percentage*
1	46/1	2.12	45/1	2.17
2	22.5/1	4.25	22/1	4.34
3	14.7/1	6.37	14.33/1	6.52
4	10.75/1	8.51	10.5/1	8.7
5	8.4/1	10.64	8.2/1	10.87
6	6.83/1	12.77	6.67/1	13.04
7	5.71/1	14.9	5.57/1	15.22
8	4.87/1	17.04	4.75/1	17.39
9	4.22/1	19.16	4.11/1	19.57
10	3.7/1	27.03	3.6/1	21.74
11	3.27/1	23.42	3.18/1	23.93
12	2.91/1	25.58	2.83/1	26.11
13	2.61/1	27.7	2.54/1	28.25
14	2.35/1	29.85	2.29/1	30.4
15	2.13/1	31.95	2.07/1	32.57
16	1.93/1	34.12	1.88/1	34.72
17	1.76/1	36.23	1.71/1	36.9
18	1.61/1	38.31	1.56/1	39.06
19	1.47/1	40.48	1.42/1	41.32
20	1.35/1	42.55	1.3/1	43.38
21	1.24/1	44.64	1.19/1	45.66
22	1.13/1	46.95	1.09/1	47.85
23	1.04/1	49.02	1/1	50
24	0.95/1	51.28	0.92/1	52.08
25	0.88/1	53.19	0.84/1	54.35

Pot odds

The pot odds are the odds that you are getting for making a bet. Before placing a bet it is helpful to know if the bet is worth making. You can do this by comparing the odds to achieve a particular hand, with the pot odds. For example: if there is £50 in the pot and you need to make a bet of £5 to stay in the game, you are getting odds of 50/5, or 10/1.

To make a bet worthwhile, the pot odds would need to be higher than the odds of achieving a winning hand. Suppose the pot odds are 10/1 and the odds of you making a hand that you assess is sufficient to win are 4/1, it is worth betting. If, however, the pot odds are 8/1 and the odds of you achieving a winning hand are 14/1, then it is not worth betting.

EXAMPLE 1

Pocket cards: Ks, 10s

Flop: 5s, 2s, Jd

If your pocket cards are two spades and the flop gives two spades, you have a chance of making a flush with spades. There are 13 spades in total. Four of them have been dealt – two to your hand and two to the flop. There are nine left in the deck (13 – 4 = 9).

This gives you nine outs.

Using the formula given above (9 × 2) = 18 per cent.

You therefore have approximately an 18-per-cent chance of making the flush. Your bet should be no more than 18 per cent of the pot value. If there is £200 in the pot: £200 × 18/100 = £36. Your bet should be less than £36 to be worthwhile.

EXAMPLE 2

You have a pair of kings and want to calculate your chances of getting a third king. There are four kings; you have two, which leaves two in the deck. You therefore have two outs.

Using the formula above, (2 × 2) = 4 per cent. You therefore have approximately a 4-per-cent chance of making the three of a kind. Your bet should be no more than 4 per cent of the pot value. If there is £100 in the pot, your bet should be less than £4 to be worthwhile. If you need to bet, for example, £10 to stay in the game, it would be better to fold.

Test your knowledge (answers at the back)

1 Calculate your chances of being dealt pocket kings.

2 Pocket cards: Jd, Jc; community cards: Jh, 8d, Ks. How many outs do you have for making four of a kind?

3 Pocket cards: Kh, 7h; community cards: Jh, 6h, Ad. How many outs do you have for making a flush?

4 Pocket cards: Kd, Kh. What are your odds of improving to three of a kind with three kings on the flop?

5 If you have nine outs on the flop, what is your approximate percentage chance of improving on the turn?

6 If you have four outs on the turn, what is your approximate percentage chance of improving your hand on the river?

7 If you have two outs on the flop, what is your approximate percentage chance of improving on the turn?

8 There is £200 in the pot. You have a 4-per-cent chance of making a high-ranking hand. You need to bet £50 to stay in the game. Is it worth betting?

9 There is £25 in the pot. You need to bet £5 to stay in the game. You have odds of 4/1 against getting a high-ranking hand. Is it worth betting?

10 There is £100 in the pot. You need to bet £10 to stay in the game. You have odds of 20/1 against getting a high-ranking hand. Is it worth betting?

Next step

You should now have a good appreciation of the chances of making ranking hands. In the following chapter you will learn about bluffing. Bluffing allows you to win a game of poker even though you may be holding a poor hand. You will learn how often to bluff and when it is an opportune moment to bluff. You will also be taught how to spot when other players are bluffing. This skill will help you to increase your winnings.

5

Bluffing

In this chapter you will learn:

▶ *What bluffing and semi-bluffing are*
▶ *When to bluff*
▶ *How often you should bluff*
▶ *How to spot when other players are bluffing*
▶ *Tips for controlling your body language*
▶ *How to assess the competition*
▶ *How to spot tells in games without webcams*
▶ *Examples of bluffing.*

What is bluffing?

If all the other players fold in a game of poker, the remaining player wins the pot and does not have to reveal his held cards to the other players. This means that it is possible to win a game without necessarily having the best hand. Bluffing is convincing the other players that you have a good hand when you actually have a poor hand.

Bluffing is achieved by placing big bets to intimidate the other players to fold. The advantage of bluffing is that it allows you to attempt to win a pot even when the cards that you have are poor in value and would have little chance of winning in a showdown. To succeed with a bluff, you need to raise the betting to a level high enough to ensure that the players fold before the game reaches a showdown. If your bluff is successful, you will win the pot and no one will know that you were bluffing. If, however, you are forced into a showdown, you must reveal your cards and your bluff will have failed.

Semi-bluffing

Semi-bluffing is making a big bet when your current hand is poor but has a good opportunity to improve to a good hand. Your initial cards may not be enough to win a game, but if you stay in until more cards are revealed you may get what you want to make a great hand. If you don't get the cards you want, then you continue to play out the hand as if they are there. You may, for example, have two cards for a potential straight or flush that are low in value. After the flop, you still need two cards to make a straight. You continue playing as if the flop has given you what you needed for a good hand. By sufficiently raising the stakes you attempt to make the others fold. If this does not work, you continue to bet and hope that you get your necessary cards.

When should you bluff?

Bluffing does not work for all games. Bluffing is ineffective in low-stake games. Players will tend to stay in if it doesn't cost too much to continue playing. An extra chip or two when the chips are low in value will not make much difference to someone's bankroll.

Bluffing is most effective in high-stake games where it is possible to substantially increase bets. If it becomes expensive for a player to stay in a game, they are more likely to consider folding. Bluffing is particularly suited to no-limit Texas hold 'em because you can make a bet that is big enough to make anyone think twice before continuing to play.

The size of the pot will influence your decision on whether or not to bluff. Bluffing is most useful for taking small pots. In a situation where lots of players have folded, you are left with little competition for the pot. With a small pot, players are more likely to fold if they have a mediocre hand. Although they could improve, they will often prefer to sit the game out and wait for a better hand with a bigger pot. In contrast, a large pot will be much more competitive. Players will be more likely to fight for a pot where they have contributed a substantial stake.

Tournaments offer more opportunities for bluffing than normal games. This is because players tend to play tightly, taking few risks. Play is against strangers, and in the initial stages the players will want to assess their opponents. As play progresses and players get short on chips, they will want to save them for their best hands and not risk getting involved in a high round of betting that could cost them the tournament.

If you play with a regular group of players, knowing your opponents is important. You will also have an idea of the sort of hand that a particular opponent plays. Do they tend to wait for really good hands before playing or do they go with a mediocre hand and hope to improve? You will need to learn what makes them fold and what doesn't. Some players will never fold and will always stay in until the conclusion of a game. If up against such a player, you will always be involved in a showdown and, if their cards are better, will be beaten. The other players will also see that you have been trying to bluff, which will affect your credibility as a tight player. It is therefore pointless bluffing in this situation.

If you are playing with weak players, it is not worth bluffing. They are less likely to recognize that you are trying to convince them that you have a good hand. They will tend to keep betting just to stay in the game. In weak games you may also come across players who bluff practically all the time and will keep playing to a showdown.

Bluffing is best used against good players. A good player will realize that your increase in stakes means that you either have a good hand or that you are bluffing. If you have a reputation as a tight player, the increase in stakes will be taken seriously.

Remember this: Bluffing will not always work

Not every player will back down, particularly if they believe that they have a good hand. If you find yourself in the situation where your bluff is not believed, it may be better to fold earlier rather than later. If you are continually re-raised, you can quickly lose all your chips.

Ideally, you should bluff when there are just a few people left in the game. It is easier to convince one or two people that you have a good hand than it is to convince five or six.

Your position in relation to the dealer will have an influence on whether or not it is worthwhile to bluff. It is not good to bluff from an early position as you have no idea whether the other players have been dealt a good hand or not. It is much better to bluff from a late position as you will see the players' reactions to their hands and how they bet. If everyone has checked, this shows that their hands are not particularly special. It is easier to bluff when players show weakness by checking on a previous round compared to showing strength by betting.

Making a big bet can show that you have a good hand when you have nothing. The only two unknowns are the two blinds. How they bet will determine whether or not you should continue with a bluff or fold. A strong raise from one of the blinds could indicate that they have a good hand. It could equally indicate that they are also trying to bluff. You will have to use your knowledge of the players to decide your next move. If everyone folds on the first round of betting and you are left with just the two blinds, then most of the competition has been eliminated. By betting, you could convince the blinds that you have a decent hand.

A good time to bluff is when you have just won a big pot with a good hand. A forceful round of betting will be more likely to convince the other players that your luck is in and you've got another good hand.

It's important not to get caught bluffing as you will lose credibility. You need to be able to force players to fold without getting caught in a showdown. If you've recently been caught bluffing, players will tend to call your bets. You can, however, use getting caught to your advantage if, shortly after, you have a good hand. The other players will remember that you just bluffed and are more likely to assume that you are trying to pull off another bluff. You can then use this opportunity to raise your stakes and take a big pot.

You should bluff when other players are running short on chips. They are more likely to fold in order to play in the next game. You will need to take care if they stay in, though, because, if they go all-in, you will be forced to a show down. Avoid bluffing against players with lots of chips – they are more likely to carry on betting.

Bluffs that seem to present a specific hand like a flush, straight or full house have a much better chance to succeed. Trying to convince the other players that you have made a good hand will be easier. If there appears to be nothing on the board, it will be harder to convince the other players that you have anything special.

A bluff when you are on a losing streak or when you are low on chips comes across as desperation and is less likely to be believed by the other players. If you have to go all-in, you will be forced to a showdown and your bluff will be revealed and this will reduce your credibility. Your knowledge of the other players will be a help. If you are up against players who tend to fold easily, then you can pull off a bluff.

Be wary of bluffing when there are high cards in the flop like A, K, Q, J or 10, as someone will inevitably have a match and will be highly unlikely to back down. If there is an ace in the flop, there is bound to be someone who already has an ace in their hand.

Example

With a flop of A, K, J, anyone holding an ace, king or jack will stay in, and anyone with a pair of aces, pair of kings or pair of jacks will stay in. So, too, will anyone holding a queen, in the hope of getting a straight. The competition for the pot will be too great. If the board ends up as A, K, J, 10, 7, anyone with a queen knows that they have the best possible hand - the nuts. Anyone with three of a kind will probably stay in. Anyone with an ace and another high card may also stay in. Those who have just missed their hand may also stay in and attempt a bluff.

If there are low cards in the flop, it is less likely that someone will have a match. Players are much more likely to stay in with high cards. If you start betting strongly as if you have a three of a kind or a high pair, this is more likely to be believed. You need to ensure that you bet strongly enough to force out your opponents before more cards are dealt.

If you bet pre-flop and don't get the desired hand after the flop, you could continue betting as if you had got what you wanted. The players will note your strong position pre-flop and your apparently stronger position post flop.

How often should you bluff?

Every game is different and you will have to learn to judge when it is an opportune moment to bluff. Bluffing should be used sparingly. Having a good hand is more likely to win you a game than a bluff. As a rule of thumb, a bluff should be used no more than once every 20 to 30 hands.

If you watch televised poker, it may appear that bluffing is commonplace. This is due to the television companies tending to show the most exciting highlights and someone trying to pull off a bluff is more interesting to watch than an average game.

Getting caught bluffing once in a while will not have a negative effect. However, it is not good to get a reputation as a bluffer. If you constantly bluff, the other players will not be convinced when you raise the stakes and will tend to take you all the way to a showdown.

It is much better to develop the image of a tight player who bets only with a good hand and folds with a poor hand. If you then go with a bluff, you are more likely to convince the other players that you have a good hand. The other players will be wary of you raising stakes because you have a reputation for only going with the best hands.

Spotting when other players are bluffing

You will need to assess whether or not another player is bluffing or has a good hand. The sort of questions you need to ask yourself to weigh up the situation are:

▶ Is the player taking advantage of a late position?

▶ Is the pot small?

▶ Are there just a few players left?

▶ Has everyone else checked?

▶ Is the player a known bluffer?

▶ Is the player on a losing streak?

▶ Is the player taking advantage of a big win?

BODY LANGUAGE

Webcam poker allows you to see the other players. This means you are able to take into account a player's body language.

To play poker well, you need to discern what sort of hand the other players have got in order to decide whether or not your hand is worth playing. The way that a person conducts themselves in a game can give you some clues to help you make a decision. Everyone has habits, ways of behaving and physical reactions that are difficult to control. Learning to recognize these can help you to work out if a player really has a good hand or if they are bluffing. The way that an individual reacts will be personal to them, so you may see different responses to the same situation in different people.

WHAT IS A TELL?

In poker, if a player always responds in the same way to a certain situation, this is called a tell. A tell is a physical sign that gives away the hand that someone is holding. It will be a particular habit that shows when the player has a good or a bad hand. This can be the way that a player bets. They may have a set betting pattern dependent on how good their hand is. If they get a good hand, they bet in a certain way. If they bluff, they bet in a different way. It can be the way a player sits at the table, scratches their head or coughs – indeed, it can be almost any physical mannerism or tic.

Looking for tells is an aid to help you discern what a player's hand is. Using a tell to win a hand should be no substitute for good play, however. You are more likely to win with good hands, though spotting a tell will give you a slight edge.

BLUFFING AND LYING

When someone bluffs in poker they are basically lying about their hand. When people lie they may demonstrate one or more classic signs. Some people are better liars than others and can easily disguise their deception. For this reason you will have to carefully observe your opponents and try to find out whether they have any mannerisms that give them away. If a player is caught bluffing, take note of what made the bluff obvious. You may be able to use this knowledge to catch a player bluffing in a future game.

Remember this: Classic signs of lying

Some classic signs of lying are bringing the hand up to the face, covering the mouth, stroking the chin, playing with hair and crossing the arms. There are liars who will do none of these and there are people who will do all some or all of these things. Some people tend to look down when lying. A quick glance to the upper right can be a sign of lying. Others will maintain eye contact to convince you that they are not lying.

The most obvious sign that a poker player is lying is a change in behaviour. If a player is suddenly sitting very still and quiet when they were previously moving in a relaxed manner, then you need to be suspicious. The same applies if a player who was previously quiet and relaxed is now acting as if they've got a lousy hand or as if they've got a great hand. Does a player project a natural air of confidence? Is a player obviously nervous?

ANXIETY

The advantage that you have in poker is that money is at stake. This puts the players under stress and they are more likely to show signs of anxiety if they play a poor hand. When we are anxious the body has problems staying still. This may produce reactions such as the flexing of muscles, eye pupil dilation, heart palpitations and a dry throat

Things to look out for are:

- ▶ fidgeting – the player can't sit still and keeps changing position in their seat. They may smoke more than usual or have trembling hands

- ▶ a change of voice, including the pitch or stuttering

- ▶ taking more sips of a drink

- ▶ sweating

- ▶ changes in the vein on the top half of the face, indicating an increase in heart rate or blood pressure.

- ▶ licking the lips

- ▶ handling objects

- ▶ asking questions about your hand.

ACTING

Some players will start acting to give the impression that their hand is good when it is really bad and vice versa. Try to look at the player's initial reaction to their hand. A smile that is quickly replaced by a frown as the player remembers to act can tell you that the player has something good. An initial frown followed by a smile can tell you that the player has a bad hand. A player who tries to pretend that they have a lousy hand and is staying in just for fun may try too hard to convince you of their bad hand.

There are distinct differences between real expressions and feigned expressions. The face can make 5,000 expressions, so it can be difficult to work out from the face whether or not someone is lying. Poker players will try to show a neutral expression on their face – the classic poker face. There are some clues that you can look for. A fake smile will give no movement of the wrinkle lines around the eyes. Many people assume that a liar will tend to avoid eye contact, but a good liar is just as likely to look you directly in the eye. Some people will blink more when lying and others will blink less. To hide their facial expressions some poker players wear sunglasses, a cap or visor.

STANCE

The way that a player sits at the table can give away a hand. A player who slumps shows a lack of confidence and is likely to have a bad hand. A player who sits up straight when they get their cards shows that they have something good and they are getting ready to act. Increased leaning forward can be a sign that the player is bluffing.

HOW A PLAYER SPEAKS

How a player speaks can give you some clues about their hands. Liars will tend to repeat questions to give them more time to compile an answer. If you ask someone 'Have you got a good hand?' and they reply 'Have I got a good hand?', chances are they don't. Liars also tend not to use contractions: they will say 'I do not' rather than 'I don't'.

Some players will ask questions about your hand to try to get some clues. They will watch how you respond to see if you give anything away.

Leaning forward at the turn or river can mean that they are anticipating a card to make a hand that they don't yet hold.

BETTING

Look for repetitive betting patterns. A player may advertise their hand by always betting the same way with a good hand. They may bet a particular way with a mediocre hand and bet another way when bluffing.

The length of time that a player takes to make a decision can give you information. A player who takes time to make a decision after the flop may be trying to work out if they're in with a chance of making a flush or a straight.

Keep an eye on players who have folded. They will often give away information. Their reaction to the flop may indicate that they threw away a good hand that matched with their cards. If you can discern this, you will know that the chances of the other players getting a match are diminished.

Also assess how long it takes for each player to make a decision. Someone who has already decided to bluff may have worked out that they are going to bet in this round regardless of what happens. Someone who is considering bluffing may take a little time to come to a decision. Someone with a good hand will have decided that they want to bet through to the flop and will bet confidently. Someone with a mediocre hand may take time to weigh up whether or not they should bet or fold. They may hesitate while deciding whether or not to bet. Hesitation can also be used to deceive the other players. If it goes on too long, it's probably a player with a good hand feigning weakness.

Controlling your body language

A survey by Victor Chandler found that 58 per cent of poker players are looking for tells. This means that most of your opponents will be carefully watching your behaviour. In order not to give away information about your hand, you will need to make sure that you don't have any tells. If you do get caught bluffing, ask the other players how they knew it was a bluff. You may get told outright that you gave it away by fidgeting or frowning or with some other mannerism. If you are aware of your behaviour, you can modify it to disguise it.

Some pointers for controlling your body language are:

▶ Avoid acting to give out false messages about your hand. Most people are bad actors.

▶ Sit still. Avoid fidgeting, playing with chips or touching your face.

- Try to stay relaxed.

- Sit up straight.

- Quickly decide how good your hand is, what will threaten it and how you are going to play the hand.

- Bet confidently, without hesitation.

Assessing the competition

If you play against strangers, you probably won't be playing with them for long enough to spot tells. If you play regularly on a site, you will come across the same players again and again. You will have longer to study your opponents and may notice something about their behaviour that is typical to them in a particular situation. For example, they may get into the habit of always raising pre-flop when they are bluffing. They may be eager to bet without hesitation when they bluff. Not everyone will have a tell, but if you can pick out one or two players who do, you may be able to reduce the competition for the pot.

 Try it now: Keep a poker diary

Keep a diary of your opponents' habits. It may take you a few sessions to spot anything that can be useful. You may notice, for example, that a particular player always starts fidgeting when they are bluffing or that another puts on an act to feign a poor hand when they actually have a good hand. Before play, read through your diary to refresh your mind.

If you discover a tell, never reveal it to the other players. Once you know a player's weakness, you can continue to profit from it. If you reveal it to the other players, they can also exploit it. Never tell the player because they may modify their behaviour.

You can divide up players into different classes. Each type of player has a different way of reacting:

- **Strong, experienced players** will give very little away. They will likely be expressionless and will move little. Against these players you need to concentrate on playing good hands and making sure you don't give any signals about your hand.

- **Aggressive players** will try to intimidate you. They may attack with big bets or ask you questions about your hand. All of these tactics are used to make you fold rather than play. You need to learn to ignore these aggressive tactics and just play your hand. If you have a good hand worth playing, don't be scared off.

- **Novice players** are still learning and will make all kinds of mistakes. They may play a hand confidently in the wrong belief that it is a good hand. They are more likely to overact and feign the opposite hand to what they have. They will try too hard to let you believe that they have a poor hand when they actually have a good hand. They will also take their time deciding what to do.

Spotting tells in games without webcams

In many online games you can't see the players, so it is more difficult to find tells. However, there are some indications that may give you a clue. Someone who checks very quickly may have a weak hand. A fast bet on the turn or on the river can indicate a strong hand. A player who is slow to respond is likely to have a weak hand. A player who hesitates, then checks, is likely to have a weak hand. Hesitation followed by a raise shows strength. Using automatic play means that the player will have a set pattern of play. If the play suddenly changes, this probably means that the player has a good hand or is attempting a bluff. If a player is chatting, don't just ignore what they are saying – it may be relevant and could reveal a tell.

Examples of bluffing

EXAMPLE 1

Player a – 4h, 2d

Player b – Qd, Qh

Player c – Ad, Ac

Player a has a poor hand but decides to bluff.

The flop is: Js, 8s, 9s.

The flop does not help player b or c.

All players can see that there is a possible flush (five spades) or even a straight Qs, Js, 10s, 9s, 8s or Js, 10s, 9s, 8s, 7s. Player a raises, acting as if he has the cards to make one of these hands. Players b and c fold. Player a wins the pot. Both player b and c had hands that could have beaten player a in a showdown. Player a has just pulled off a successful bluff.

EXAMPLE 2

Player a – Ks, Qs

Player b – 8d, 4s

The flop is: Kh, Kd, 2d

The cards dealt on the flop may expose your bluff. With high cards in the flop there is a great chance that another player has at least one of those cards. It is better for player b to fold than to continue bluffing. Player a's pocket cards contain a king. On the flop he knows that he has three of a kind with kings and that player b cannot possibly beat him unless he is holding a pair of aces and gets another ace with the next two cards dealt. He will take player b all the way to a showdown. If player b continues to bluff, it could be a costly loss as player a continues to raise.

EXAMPLE 3

Occasionally a bluff may turn into a good hand, depending on the cards dealt.

Player a – 2h, 5h

Player b – Kh, Jc

Player c – Ad, Ac

The flop is: Ah, 4h, 3h

Player a has a poor hand that most players would normally fold on but he decides to bluff. Player b folds after the flop. Here the flop has helped player c who now has three aces. However, player a now has a straight flush: 5h, 4h, 3h, 2h, Ah. He can continue raising and force a showdown, confident that he will win the pot.

Try it now: Improving your skills

To practise when it is opportune to bluff, try dealing out practice hands. Then assess what each player would do at each stage of the game. Would your bluff be believable, or would the player likely keep playing? By doing this you can begin to assess when it is an opportune moment to fold or to continue bluffing.

Test your knowledge (answers at the back)

Is this a good time to bluff?

1 You are first to act.

2 You are last to act and there are five other players who have not folded.

3 You are last to act and there are just two players who have not folded.

4 You had a big win in the previous game.

5 You have not bluffed for at least 20 games.

6 You are playing for low stakes.

7 You are playing for high stakes.

8 You are playing in the early games of a tournament.

9 The flop contains high cards, A, K, Q or J.

10 You have spotted a tell and are certain that your opponent is bluffing.

Next step

You should now have a good understanding of the principles of bluffing – when it is opportune to bluff and when you are better folding. You should appreciate that bluffing is a strategy to use sparingly. In the next chapter you will learn further strategies that can help you to win.

6

Playing strategy

In this chapter you will learn:

- ▶ *Pocket cards strategy*
- ▶ *Pocket hands to play*
- ▶ *Pocket hands to fold on*
- ▶ *Strategy for nuts*
- ▶ *Strategies for the flop, turn and river*
- ▶ *How position affects play*
- ▶ *How to adapt your strategy for different games.*

Pocket cards strategy

The first decision you need to make is whether or not your pocket cards are worth playing. This decision will be influenced by how high your cards are, your position at the table, how many players have folded and your knowledge of the players.

Some starting hands are much better than others. In general terms, it is worthwhile playing any high pair, consecutive cards of the same suit such as Qh, Jh, Kc, Qc, and fairly high cards of the same suit such as Jd, 9d.

THE BEST POCKET HANDS

The best pocket hands are high pairs and AK suited (see Figure 6.1a). The high pairs give you the opportunity of improving your hand to a high-ranking three of a kind or four of a kind. They also open the possibility of a high-ranking full house. The A,K suited has the prospect of a flush or straight with also the possibility to improve to a high pair, two pair, three of a kind or four of a kind.

With one of these starting hands you are in a strong position from the beginning. The correct betting strategy with a hand such as this is to raise pre-flop. You can then modify your play depending on what cards you get in the flop.

Figure 6.1a The best pocket hands

GOOD POCKET HANDS

Other starting hands that are poorer than those above but worth seeing through to the flop are:

- suited high cards including A, J; K, Q; K, J; J, 10; 10, 9
- relatively high pairs such as 9, 9; 8, 8; 7, 7
- aces with a suited kicker like Ah, 10h.

See Figure 6.1b. The consecutive cards of the same suit lead to the possibility of a flush or a straight. High cards of the same suit also open the possibility for a flush or a straight. The betting strategy with these cards would be to call. If the flop fails to give an improvement then the hand should be folded.

Figure 6.1b Good pocket hands

POCKET HANDS TO FOLD

A large number of hands are of little use and are best folded.

Figure 6.1c shows some of the hands that should be folded. The following starting hands are some of the poorest hands and should be folded: 2, 6; 2, 7; 2, 8; 2, 9; 2, 10; 3, 8; 3, 9. The cards are low in value and they do not contain any pairs. Another player is likely to have higher cards. In addition, the cards are too far apart to be useful in making straights. Unsuited, they give little chance of making a flush. If you do end up with a flush, the chances are that another player may have a higher flush.

The following cards are also low in value: 3, 6; 3, 7; 4, 7; 4, 8. Other players are likely to have higher cards. Although the cards are close enough together to have the chance of making a straight, they are so low that the prospect of being beaten is high. The best move here is to fold.

High cards with an unsuited low kicker are not a good start either. This includes hands A, 2 unsuited; Q, 3 unsuited; K, 4 unsuited and J, 2 unsuited. Even if there is a match on the flop, the chances are that there is already someone with pocket pairs who could improve on the flop to three of a kind. Even a match on the flop for the kicker is a poor hand. There is highly likely to be someone with a better pair. The best move here is to fold.

The faster that you can recognize a poor hand and fold, the better. Being highly selective with the hands you play will save you more money in the long run. Placing too many bets on poor hands is a costly strategy.

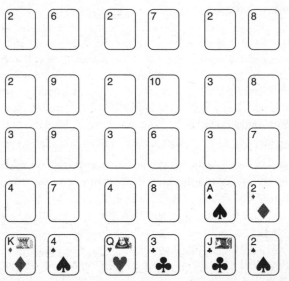

Figure 6.1c Hand to fold

How position affects play

Table position is important. In the first betting round the big blind is the last to act. In the subsequent betting rounds the dealer is the last to act. It is advantageous to be the last to act. This is because you can see what everyone's actions are before you decide what to do. You find out who is still remaining in the game. If lots of the players have already dropped out, this gives you the option to take a chance on a less good hand or to pull off a bluff. Your knowledge of the players will also allow you to assess what you need to do to eliminate the remaining players. Be aware that good players will recognize that you are playing from the last position and may take this into consideration when considering whether or not you are bluffing.

Whether or not playing lower-value hands is worthwhile can also depend on the situation. Your position at the table in relation to the last to bet and how many players before you have folded should have an influence on the hands that you play.

If you are in an early position, you definitely want to be playing one of the better hands. However, in a late position you have more options. In a late position you get to see the other players' actions. You know who has raised because they have a strong hand, who has called, and how many players have folded. You will know if you have just one or two opponents or many. If you are acting at a late position and most of the players have dropped out, you can decide to play lower-value cards. The fewer the number of players, the easier it is to win. There is less competition for each pot.

This may also be an opportune moment to pull off a bluff. A bluff from a late position with only one or two players left is more likely to succeed than a bluff from an early position with several opponents.

In a late position with few opponents, it is worth playing a low pair such as 2, 2; 3, 3; 4, 4; 5, 5 or 6, 6 (see Figure 6.2). With these hands you would definitely want to see the flop. These hands can be used as a semi-bluff. If you have the luck to get a match on the flop you can continue playing. If high cards come on the flop then folding or continuing to bluff are your options.

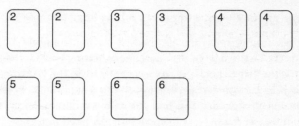

Figure 6.2 Hands to play from a late position

Your knowledge of the players will also be important. A tight player who raises from an early position will be a sign for you to be cautious. If you are aware that this is a player who will continuing raising to the showdown and is likely to reach the showdown with a good hand, you can then decide to fold.

The worst position to play from is the small blind. From the flop onwards you are the first to take action. You have no idea how the other players are going to react. Ideally, you should only stay in the action if you have a really good hand. You need to make up your mind about what you are going to do before the flop. This will mean basing your decision on the pocket cards. If your pocket cards are poor, you should fold. For some players this can be a difficult decision as the fact that they have contributed to the pot via the small blind makes them want to recoup that investment. However, getting out of the game early is a better strategy.

Strategy after the flop

Once the flop has been dealt, you have a better indication of the possible hands. You can assess your position against all the other possibilities. You need to judge how good your hand now is. If the community cards have not helped you, they may well have given other players the possibility of a really good hand. If you think that this is the situation, then fold now. There is a general rule that says: if you don't improve on the flop, you should fold. However, there are situations when you should ignore this rule. For example, if you have a pair that fails to match but all the other cards on the flop are low cards, the chances are that no one improved on the flop. You may still be in a good position and will want to see the turn.

If you have a good hand after the flop, then you don't want too many other players getting to see the turn and river cards cheaply. If they get lucky, they could beat you. This is where you need to judge how much to raise the betting by, to get the competition to fold.

EXAMPLE 1

Pocket cards: 9s, 9c

Flop: Ah, Qh, Jh

Here the hand pre-flop was a pair of 9s. The flop has not improved the hand. The flop consists of cards that are higher in value than a 9. The chances are that someone has stayed in with an ace or a queen or a jack. Anyone who now has a pair of aces, a pair of queens or a pair of jacks has already beaten the hand with a pair of 9s. Someone may also now have three aces, three queens or three jacks. Again, the pair of 9s would have been beaten. Since all the community cards are hearts, this opens the possibility of a flush or a straight. With a pair of 9s that have no chance of the flush it is advisable to fold.

EXAMPLE 2

Pocket cards: 9s, 9c

Flop: 7s, 2d, 9h

Here the flop has helped the hand. It has now improved to three of a kind and is currently the highest hand. It can improve to four of a kind or to a full house. Anyone with a high-value pair such as A, A or K, K has failed to improve. There is also little hope for a flush. The player should raise.

EXAMPLE 3

Pocket cards: Ad, Ah

Flop: Kd, Kc, Qs

What starts out as a high hand can change on the flop. Here the player started with one of the strongest hands of two aces. However, the flop has given high cards. The player with the aces is not necessarily in the strongest position. A player with pocket kings already has four of a kind. A player with pocket Q, Q or K, Q has a full house. A player with one K has three of a kind with the prospect of making a full house or four of a kind. A player with any pair also has the opportunity of making a full house. There is a high chance that one of the players has at least one king, as a king is a card that a player will tend to play regardless of what the kicker is. The player with the pair of aces is therefore likely to be at a disadvantage.

The decision you make will depend on how many players are left and what happened in the previous betting round. The previous betting round should give you an indication of the hands. Did any of the players show strength in the previous betting round by raising? You would expect anyone with a pair of kings to raise. If they now show strength by raising, it would be a better option to fold. Although it may be hard to fold on a pair of aces, it is likely to be a better option.

EXAMPLE 4

Pocket cards: Kd, Kc

Flop: 7d, 4h, 2s

Here the flop has failed to improve the pair of kings. However, the cards are all low. It is unlikely that any of the other players have been helped by the flop. The cards are all different suits, making a flush harder to achieve. The cards are also too far apart to be useful for a straight. Here you would need to consider how the other players bet in the first round. Anyone who raised should be treated with caution as they could possibly have pocket aces. However, if the first round of betting was passive, then the pocket kings could be the highest hand. If you believe this to be the case, you should raise and continue to the turn, then reassess your options.

EXAMPLE 5

> *Pocket cards:* 5d, 5h

> *Flop:* 8s, 5c, 2h

If you are in an early position, then a low pair is normally not worth playing. However, a late position allows you to play low cards when most of the competition has been eliminated. Here the flop has improved the hand to three of a kind with 5s. The only danger would come from someone with three of a kind with 8s. The cards are of different suits, so it doesn't help anyone looking for a flush or a straight. You are still in a fairly good position. You now need to eliminate as much competition as possible. Another player may hold a high pair like a pair of kings or queens. You need to raise to get them out of the game. If they stay in, they could improve to three kings or three queens, which would beat you on a showdown.

EXAMPLE 6

> *Pocket cards:* 2d, 8s

> *Flop:* Ac, 10c, 4c

The hand is poor with low unsuited cards, which should be folded when playing in an early position. However, in a late position with few players left in the game a bluff may be attempted. Raising pre-flop shows strength. At the flop the hand is still poor. However, the cards on the flop are all the same suit, giving rise to a possible flush. Anyone with pocket aces will know that, with three of a kind, they have been beaten by a flush. The most successful bluffs are when a player appears to act as if they have a particular hand. The player continues to raise as if the flush has been made. You need to raise to a sufficient enough level to ensure that the other players fold before reaching the showdown. Your knowledge of the players should help you decide how much of a raise will be sufficient. If the other players fold before the showdown, then the bluff would have worked. If they don't fold, then you would need to fold before being exposed in the showdown.

Strategy for nuts

As mentioned in Chapter 2, nuts is the best possible hand in a game. As most of the cards are revealed face up in hold 'em, it is possible to deduce what the best possible hand could be. Occasionally, a situation may arise where you know that you have the best possible hand (nuts) that can be made using the community cards. There is no way that you can be beaten. Clearly, in this situation you want to maximize the pot. Your strategy for betting will need to be based on your knowledge of the players. You need to keep the betting at the right level, to keep as many of the players betting for as long as possible.

Suppose you have Ah, Jh, and the flop is Kh, Qh, 10h; you know at this stage that you have a straight flush.

Pocket cards   Community cards

It is the best possible hand and no one else can beat you. Chances are someone else will have at least a pair of kings or a pair of queens. You don't need to force anyone out of the game. It doesn't matter how many people stay in until the showdown because you will win it. You have two choices. You can slow-play your hand, letting the other players take the initiative in raising and calling until the last betting round. You then raise when you reach the final betting round. Anyone who has paid to get this far will likely want to stay in to the showdown.

Alternatively, you can start raising on the flop. Anyone with a king or a queen will probably stay in with the hope of improving. Anyone with an ace will stay in, hoping to get a straight. They know that there is a possibility of a royal flush but will understand that the chances of anyone making it are rare. If you raise now, chances are that they will still stay in to the showdown. The pot that you win will therefore be much greater than a hand that was slow-played. The option that you take will depend on your knowledge of the players and their actions.

You may not know that you have nuts until all the community cards have been dealt:

EXAMPLE 1

Pocket cards   Community cards

Here the player does not get nuts until all of the community cards are dealt. Then he can see that he has the straight Q, J, 10, 9, 8. This is the best possible hand that could be made with the cards shown. A player with, for example, three jacks would lose against him in a showdown. A flush is not possible because there are not three cards of the same suit in the community cards.

In this game a number of players may have stayed in. The flop of 4, 2, J was nothing special. Anyone with a high pair would likely stay in. The jack helps the player with Q, 9. The straight needs a 10, and any king or any eight will complete it. After the next card, the 10 is there. The player now knows that he needs any king or any 8. An 8 appears on the river.

EXAMPLE 2

Pocket cards   Community cards

In this example the player has three kings – the best possible hand. The third king comes in the flop. You have two choices: you can either slow-play the hand or start raising. If you slow-play, you take the risk that anyone with pocket 8s or pocket 6s will likely go all the way to the showdown and may get a fourth card on the way. A player with pocket aces is likely to stay in to the river, hoping to get another ace. It is therefore a better strategy to start raising. A raise may help to cut the competition. Even if it fails to cut the competition, it will maximize the pot.

Strategy on the turn

By the turn there may be players who have already made a good hand on the flop. Others will have a potentially good hand that still needs one or two cards to complete it. If they fail to get the desired cards on the turn and river, they will have nothing. Others may have a mediocre hand that they are still hoping to improve. Another player may simply be bluffing.

If you are still playing by the turn, you should either have a good hand or the potential to make a good hand on the draw. If you think you have the best hand, you should be raising to try to get the other players to fold before they have the chance to improve. A player who still needs a card to complete a hand will be more likely to fold if it costs too much to stay in the game. Your knowledge of the players should give you an indication of how much you need to bet to get a particular player to fold.

If you have committed to the turn because you need one more card for your hand, then you should stay for the river if it is not too expensive. If the stakes go too high, you should fold.

Strategy on the river

Any players left at the river now know exactly what their hands are. They can also analyse what the possibilities are for the other player's hands. If you think yours is best, you should raise to try to get as much money as possible out of your opponents. This is your last opportunity to increase the pot. If you needed a card to complete your hand and failed to get it, and it looks as though your opponents will take you to a showdown, you should fold. If you think that you have been beaten, it is best to fold rather than be dragged into a raising battle.

Betting strategy

Betting is used to force other players to fold. It is also used to entice other players to bet more than they had intended, to maximize the pot. Using the correct strategy can greatly increase the amount won. A good knowledge of the odds can help you to ensure that the opponents make bets that are unprofitable for them. Different types of games require different betting strategies.

If you have a good hand, checking or calling is a poor strategy. If everyone else checks, you have just wasted an opportunity to get more money into the pot and given the other players a cheap look at more cards where they could improve their hands. It is much better to make a bet or a raise so that everyone else is forced to pay, in order to stay in the game. With one of the best starting hands the best strategy is to raise. You want to try to get as much money as possible into the pot.

Showing strength can be a better strategy than showing weakness. More aggressive play can be intimidating for some players and can help to make them fold hands that they could potentially improve and win in a showdown.

FIXED-LIMIT
Here the increase in stakes is relatively small. Often, it is not possible to force players to back down, simply because it costs so little to go all the way to the river. More often than not, players will end up in showdowns. This makes it much more difficult to pull off a bluff as you are not able to back up the bluff with a large enough bet. In these games position must be used to the utmost if you want to pull off a bluff. Acting last is the most opportune moment to bluff with the use of aggressive play. Raising from the start of the game will be necessary.

With a good hand you need to be raising to get maximum value. Because the other players are likely to go all the way to the showdown, you need to get as much money as possible in the pot.

Playing tightly should enable you to win more pots. Only play good hands that have a realistic chance of winning. If you believe you have the best hand, you should be raising from the start. The more money that comes into the pot, the greater your win will be. There will be other players who will call your bets as they will be reluctant to fold before the flop. Even if they fail to improve on the flop, some players will not fold simply because they have already contributed so much to the pot when matching your raises. If you continue raising post flop, you are likely to scare off some players while others will continue to the showdown, still hoping to improve. Your knowledge of the players will help you here. You should have a good idea of their playing methods.

POT-LIMIT AND NO-LIMIT GAMES

Pot-limit and no-limit games give you the opportunity to make much bigger bets than fixed-limit games. Pot-limit games allow you to raise up to the value of the current pot. With no-limit games the maximum amount that you can bet or raise is the total value of your chips on the table.

Because players are able to bet so much in these games, it is important to make sure that bets are the correct size at each stage. Bets should be proportional to the current pot. If you believe that you have the best hand, you should bet at least three-quarters of the pot or as much as you think you could reasonably bet that will not force your opponents to fold. You want them to keep on calling your bets. Your knowledge of the players will help you to make the right-size bet.

If your hand is really strong after the flop, you should play aggressively and raise. You need to eliminate anyone who may improve on the turn.

Betting can also be used to buy yourself a better position. Being last to act is the best position to have. If you are a couple of players away from the last, a large raise can force out the last few players.

Using the odds to decide action

In pot-limit and no-limit games you should be calculating the odds to decide what the best action to take is. The strategy here is to make bets of a sufficient enough size that you give your opponents poor odds to stay in the game.

EXAMPLE 1

Pocket cards: Ac, Ah

Flop: Kd, Qd, 3s

The pair of aces is one of the best starting hands. However, it has not been helped by the flop. It is still the highest pair and has the chance of improving on the turn or river to three of a kind. You can see that there is a possible flush. A player holding two diamonds will have a 35-per-cent chance of making the flush. To discourage a player from trying to make the flush, you need to size your bet correctly:

▷ If the pot is currently 500, a bet of 800 would bring the pot to 1,300, giving him odds of 1,300/800 = 1.625/1, or 38 per cent, to call the bet. This is a good-value bet for the player.

▷ If, instead, you raise the bet to 1,000, the pot would be 1,500. He would need to call 1,000. The odds become 1,500/1,000 = 15/1, or 6.25 per cent.

EXAMPLE 2

Pocket cards: Kh, Kd

Flop: Jh, Ks, 10h

You can also assess how good your hand is by analysing the hand and calculating the number of outs that a player could have compared to you. The hand is currently three of a kind with kings. There is one out, for a four of a kind with kings on the turn. There is also the possibility of a full house. There are six outs for the full house – three jacks and three 10s. There are also ten outs for the flush, with the possibility of a royal flush. There is also the possibility of a straight with an ace and a queen, giving an additional six outs. In total, there are 23 outs.

If another player has two pocket cards to the flush, they hold four cards to a flush. The fact that you are holding the king of hearts stops them from getting a royal flush. They have only eight outs for a flush but could have a higher flush with the Ah as a pocket card.

If a player is holding A, A, they have just two outs to get a third ace on the turn.

Anyone matching the jacks or the 10s already has a lower hand. They will have just one out, to get the four of a kind on the turn.

If a player is holding A, Q as pocket cards, they already have the highest straight. However, it can't be improved. Ignoring the straight, you still have 17 outs for a better hand.

Test your knowledge (answers at the back)

Should you play or fold the following hands?

1 Pocket cards: Ad, Ah

2 Pocket cards: 7d, 2c

3 Pocket cards: Kd, Jd

4 Pocket cards: 9s, 3c

5 Pocket cards: 10h, 9h

6 Pocket cards: Qs, Qc

7 Pocket cards: 8c, 4c

8 Pocket cards: As, Ks

9 Pocket cards: 9d, 9c

10 Pocket cards: 2s, 2d

11 Pocket cards: 10h, 10c

Flop: 7s, 2d, 10h

12 Pocket cards: 4d, 4h

Flop: 6s, 4c, 2h

You are in a late position with only one other opponent. Should you play or fold the following hands?

13 Pocket cards: Ad, As

Flop: 5d, 9c, 2h

14 Pocket cards: Qd, Jd

Flop: Ah, As, 7c

15 Pocket cards Jh, Jc

Flop: Jd, 4c, Js

More questions

16 You have reached the turn and failed to get the final card needed for a flush. No one has raised. Should you stay for the river?

17 You believe you have the best hand after the flop. Should you raise?

18 You have reached the river with a bluff and your opponent has continued to raise. Should you call or fold?

19 Your opponent has a 35-per-cent chance of making a flush. There is currently £1,000 in the pot. Would a bet of £200 be enough to make it unprofitable for him to call?

20 Your opponent has a 35-per-cent chance of making a flush. There is currently £100 in the pot. Would a bet of £80 be enough to make it unprofitable for him to call?

Next step

In the following chapter you will build upon your knowledge of strategy and learn how to become a better player. You will learn how to categorize other players and analyse your results. Table position will be discussed in greater detail. You will also learn how to avoid the mistakes that beginners typically make.

7

Becoming a better player

In this chapter you will learn:

▶ *How to practise the game*
▶ *How to avoid beginner's mistakes*
▶ *How to improve your play*
▶ *How games vary*
▶ *How to assess other players*
▶ *About keeping records*
▶ *How to analyse hands.*

Practising offline

Before going online you should start training yourself with a pack of cards. It is helpful to deal out imaginary games, because in a real game you will not get to see the other player's pocket cards unless they reach the showdown. By dealing imaginary games, you can compare your actions to what the other players would have done and then assess your cards against theirs.

As a beginner, you will start out on fixed-limit games where you will often end up in a showdown. It is therefore important to play out your best hands. You will want to ensure that you reach the showdown with a good hand that has a realistic chance of winning.

Try it now: Practice hands

Deal out ten sets of pocket cards. Look at each set and decide if you would play or fold them. Then deal out the community cards and assess whether or not you made a good decision. Are you throwing away cards that could have won? Are you deciding to play cards that have no hope of winning? By continually doing this you will get a better idea of the sort of hands that have a better chance of winning.

When you are proficient enough to pick out good pocket cards, move on to practising what you would do on the flop. Play the hand through to the river. Record whether or not you made a good decision. This will help you assess whether or not you are playing hands that have a good chance of winning or losing.

When you have mastered what to do on the flop, your next challenge is the turn and the river. Take the time to practise whether or not you should fold or play. Record your decisions and assess the results.

The online poker sites have videos of games that you can watch. You should spend some time studying these games. This will help you get used to the betting system and the way that the game is dealt. At first, it may seem that the games are going too fast but as you get used to the action you will be able to keep up.

It is important that you gain knowledge and experience. The more knowledgeable you are about the game the better. Read about the game. Try out various playing strategies and see what works best for you.

If you are happy with your play and understand all aspects of the game, you can then try out free games online. The online poker sites allow you to practise without betting any money. Playing free games online will give you valuable experience. Just getting used to the layout of a site can take some time to master. The free games will allow you to practise betting and you will learn how other players act.

Remember this: Play at the correct level

When you decide that you are ready to play for real money, start with low-stake fixed-limit games. This will help you to minimize losses. When you are confident at one level and are playing well and winning, you can consider moving up to the next level. If your move up a level is failing and you start losing too much, then you should drop back down and get more practice at the previous level. Don't be in too much of a rush to reach the top tables. The players there will have plenty of experience.

Avoid beginner's mistakes

▶ **Don't try to play every hand.** You need to appreciate that it is impossible to win every hand. The hands that you do play need to be carefully selected. You will need the patience to throw away poor hands and wait until you are dealt a good starting hand. Continually trying to play poor hands will lose you money. Folding as soon as possible is a good strategy for saving money. Staying in for one more bet with a long shot will cost you money.

▶ **Don't overestimate the value of pocket cards.** Many players make the mistake of assuming that a court card or an ace in a hand is automatically a good hand. Unless the second card is sufficiently high or suited, then the hand is not a good starting hand.

- **Use bluffing sparingly.** You need to carefully time a bluff. If you are seen as a player who rarely bluffs you will be able to scare off players who could beat you. Getting caught bluffing is bad for your reputation.

- **Understand the odds** and learn how to bet in a strategic manner and be able to assess the other player's strengths and weaknesses. You will need to be able to adapt your strategies to compensate for the other players and also to be unpredictable.

- **Concentrate on the game.** Avoid multi-playing (playing several games at once), because you will miss crucial information about players and their betting patterns. At the same time you should take advantage of multi-players as they will be paying less attention to individual games.

Remember this: Use aggressive play judiciously

Being aggressive against weak players is a good tactic. However, it will not work with skilled players. By assessing the players you can work out who is weak and inexperienced.

The number of players

The number and experience of the players will have an influence on the strategy that you need to use. With a large number of players you need to bear in mind that the competition for a good hand will be greater and there is a greater likelihood that one of the players is going to have a good hand. Where there are lots of players and you have a decent hand, you need to try to cut down the competition as early as possible to ensure that those with mediocre hands fold before they get the opportunity to improve. If you are playing with less experienced players, they are more likely to stay in the game for longer and not fold. In such games you need to be certain that you are playing a good hand that has a very good chance in a showdown, because you are much more likely to end up in showdowns.

You will need to modify your strategy in games where there are fewer players. In games with, for example, six players it is possible to play more loosely than in games with ten players.

You can play lower starting hands because the chance of getting good starting hands will be cut. If you play heads-up games where there are just two players, you will need to start playing virtually every hand. This is because in every game you will be making either a small blind or a big blind bet.

How playing online differs from live play

You will often be playing with strangers instead of people you know well. Playing online has advantages and disadvantages over live play. With the vast majority of games there is no physical contact between the players. You cannot see them and they cannot see you. This means you do not have to worry about keeping a poker face and paying attention to your body language. This also means that you cannot assess other players' body language and look for tells.

Because you cannot see the players, you need to develop a different strategy for playing. The strategy used needs to be based more on probabilities, betting patterns and knowledge gained from previous games with players that you may encounter in the future. If you often play on the same site, you may regularly play with the same players and build up a body of information about the habits and betting patterns of these players. Some sites offer games via web cameras. These games will be more like traditional games where you can see the players. In this case, it is important not to give the other players subtle information that could help them to deduce your likely hand and whether or not you are bluffing.

Keeping records

Keep records of your gambling. Most sites allow you to go back over your hands and will give you an analysis of how many games you have lost or won, your stakes and how profitable your play has been. Most people tend to remember the big wins and forget the losses. Analyse the results and learn from your mistakes:

▶ If you lost, try to determine why. Were you staying in when you should have folded? Were you folding with hands that could have won? Were you failing to force other players into folding? Were your actions giving away information?

▶ When you win, also try to determine the reasons why. Was it because your strategy was good? Were you just dealt lots of good hands? Did other players make stupid mistakes? Were you picking up on any signs given by the other players?

Periodically analyse your records. These will tell you if you're sticking to your budget and if your betting strategy is effective. Proper records will make you aware of any weaknesses. You can then alter your strategy to compensate.

Assessing the other players

Assessing the other players can help you to win more. You will find all levels of player online, from experts to complete novices. Some players may be reckless. Try to identify who you are up against. Keep records of each player that you come up against. You are bound to meet them again in another game. Any knowledge you have from the start will give you an advantage over the other players. If you play regularly with the same people, try to build up a profile of each one.

There are limits, however, to how far you can go in assessing the players. It is not permissible to use data-mining techniques in which software is used to track literally thousands of players and build up incredibly detailed records. Poker sites actively look for players who do this. You have to load a site's software on to your computer in order to play, so, if you have any banned software on your computer, they can detect it.

Any information that you hold on other players that you have found out in the normal course of play is acceptable.

The sort of information you want to know includes:

▶ Is the player a beginner or experienced?

▶ Is the player skilful?

▶ How do they bet with a good hand?

▶ What sort of hands do they bet heavily on?

▶ What forces them to fold?

▶ How often do they bluff?

- Do their actions give any clues?

- Is there any kind of a pattern to their betting?

- Do they ignore position? (Some players do not appreciate
  the finer aspects of the game and do not realize that there are
  advantages and disadvantages to position.)

IDENTIFYING MULTI-PLAYERS

When you go to the lobby you have the chance to look around
the various tables. Pick out the type of game and stake levels
that interest you. Note the names of the other players. Then
take a look around to find out whether any of the players are
also playing on other tables (multi-playing). Note how many
tables they are playing. Those who are playing lots of tables
will often be playing their highest pocket cards. They may have
eight or twenty games on the go at once. The larger the number
of games that they are playing, the less attention they will be
giving to individual games. Anyone who is playing just one
table is more likely to be a beginner or less experienced.

WHAT IS THE ONLINE STATUS OF A PLAYER?

Some sites will rank the players with, for instance, stars or other
symbols that identify them as VIPs or professionals, which will
give you information about whether or not they are regular and
experienced players. The chat boxes can also give you clues.
Players that have been playing for a long time will have built up
relationships with other players; this is something you can glean
from their conversations.

NUMBER OF HANDS PLAYED

You will want to identify how many hands a player is folding.
Those who fold the most are tight players who will only play
high-ranking pocket hands. For each game, record who is
playing and who folds. After a number of games you will find
who is playing too many hands and who is playing tightly.

SHOWDOWNS

Showdowns can tell you a lot about players. What pocket cards
did they have that they decided to play? This can tell you whether
they play only good cards or have a tendency to play anything.

Was this a player with lousy pocket cards who just got lucky? Or did they play a tight game? Make notes – you can use this information in later games.

Categorizing the players

Poker is as much about predicting the actions of others as playing the odds. Players use different styles of play. Some play aggressively, continually raising in an attempt to force everyone to fold. Other players are very cautious, throwing away anything that is not a good hand. You will know when they suddenly make a huge bet that they have a good hand. Try to work out each player's strategy. Other players are clueless and will play every hand thinking that they always have a chance of winning.

▶ **Rocks or tight players** These will fold poor pocket hands and play only when they have a good starting hand. Their play is entirely predictable. As soon as they start raising you know that they have a good hand.

▶ **Loose players** These will play lots of hands – good and bad. Loose play is typical for beginners who think that they can win whatever hand they hold. They will tend to stay in the betting for too long and are loath to fold until they see all of the community cards. Other loose players will just be playing for fun and will have made no serious study of strategy.

▶ **Aggressive players** These will play more hands than tight players. They will raise from the outset and continue raising in order to intimidate players into folding. They will play hands both good and bad with the intention of raising the stakes to a high enough level to force players into folding.

▶ **Limpers** These players will take no initiative. They will rarely raise and tend to check and call their way through a game. Much like loose players, they will stay in a game for too long. They will often stay to a showdown unless the stakes become too high.

▶ **Multi-players** These will be playing many games at once. This means that they will be concentrating less on their games. Because they are playing so many games, they will make quick decisions. A multi-player who suddenly takes more time to make a decision may have a good hand or, alternatively, be concentrating more on another table.

▶ **Drunk players** These will be totally reckless. They will take lots of risks and make stupid mistakes. They will play just about any hand and lose most of them.

▶ **Emotional players** Some players will let their emotions get the better of them. They may get angry at a big loss or a losing streak and start to play in a more reckless and aggressive way.

Your table image

The image that you adopt at the table will influence how the other players react to you. It can be good initially to come across as a tight player. Once this image is accepted by the other players, you can then play more loosely. If you then act aggressively, you should find players folding when you want them to. Try not to stick to one style of playing. The most successful poker players are those who are totally unpredictable. If in some hands you play cautiously and in others aggressively, you will confuse the opposition. You will need to adapt your play to the game and to the competition. There are no hard-and-fast rules about what to do. Every game is different and you need to adapt your play to suit that game and the players whom you are up against.

Betting strategy

Be clear about how you should be betting. Ensure that you have a strategy. Take full advantage of good hands. Don't call when you should be raising. Don't be intimidated by aggressive players. If you believe that you have the best hand, then you should re-raise aggressive players. They will likely be playing a lower hand. If they want to reach the showdown, you should make them pay for the privilege.

In order to make a proper assessment of your hand, you really need to see all of the community cards first. However, if you always stay in the game until all of the community cards have been dealt, in the long run you will lose money. The trick with hold 'em is to learn to fold early when your hand shows little promise and only continue to the showdown with good hands.

Remember this: Appreciate your chances of winning

Many people expect to win but don't realistically assess their chances of winning. With all bets there is the chance that you will lose, and it is important to understand how to calculate your chances of winning. You may decide that a bet is simply not worthwhile.

Learn how to calculate the odds for the game that you are playing. Learn how to calculate the chances of getting your desired hand and compare this with the stakes you bet, the potential pot and the chances of other hands beating yours. Fully appreciate your chances of improving hands. Before you place a bet, make sure you understand your chances of winning and losing.

Body language

Some sites have introduced webcam games. This introduces a whole new dimension to online play, making it more like an offline experience. Here body language comes into play and bluffing takes on a whole new dimension.

Suppose you have a really good hand. It is quite likely that, as you look at the cards, you will smile, raise your eyebrows or constantly look at your cards. You know that this time you are certain of a winning hand. When you're anxious or excited your voice also changes. The other player will notice and probably fold, meaning that your good hand will win you very little money.

If, alternatively, you have a poor hand, you are more likely to frown. You may decide to try bluffing, but, if you appear nervous or fidgety, the other players are less likely to believe you. You may even give one of the classic signs of lying, such as touching your nose. When you are nervous you are also more likely to stutter.

People who have complete control over their mannerisms make better poker players. If you can look at your cards and show no facial expression whatsoever, you make it impossible for other players to glean any information about your hand. When you look at your hand, memorize its contents. Pay attention to your mannerisms – don't fiddle with your chips or your jewellery. Stay calm, even if you have a royal flush. If you play and bet confidently, you are more likely to intimidate the other players. See Chapter 5 for a more detailed look at body language.

Learning to analyse the hands

You should analyse the community cards to deduce what the other players' hands could be. Consider what the various alternatives are. Which hands would be a threat to your hand? Then use your knowledge of the odds to calculate the chances of another player having that hand compared to the chances of you making yours.

EXAMPLE

Community cards

The best possible hand from the community cards showing is four of a kind with aces, followed by a full house, then a flush, and then three of a kind.

On the flop, player a will deduce that he has a good hand with three of a kind with aces. He knows that he has the best possible three of a kind. If someone else has an ace, they could also have the same three of a kind. Player a also has a high kicker with the chance of improving to a full house. He knows that he can be beaten by a full house and since he holds one of the aces, the chances of anyone holding another ace are low. By the river, to complete a full house someone would need either two queens, two 4s or two 3s, or to have the other ace with a queen, 4 or 3.

Player b started off with a low pocket hand of a pair of 3s. The intention would have been to semi-bluff. On the flop the hand has improved to a full house. The semi-bluff has turned into a really good hand. He will appreciate that there could be someone with a higher pair who would currently have two pair with a chance of improving to a full house that could potentially beat his hand. By the turn, he can be more confident in his hand as the four of diamonds is a low card that is highly unlikely to have helped anyone. By the river, he knows that only four of a kind or a full house with queens or fours could beat him.

At the flop, player c has nothing and would be wise to fold. Two aces are in the flop, which makes it highly likely that someone will have matched the aces because players tend to play aces regardless of what their other card is.

If player a and b both reach the showdown, b would win.

Test your knowledge (answers at the back)

1 As a beginner, should you play fixed-limit or no-limit games?

2 Should you try to win every hand in a game with ten players?

3 There are six players. Should you play more loosely or more tightly than you would in a game with ten players?

4 A player folds more often than other players. Is he a tight or loose player?

5 Should you try to win every hand in a heads-up game?

6 Should you multi-play?

7 Should you always play with an ace in your hand?

8 In a fixed-limit game, are you more or less likely to end in a showdown?

9 Should you try to work out what your opponents' hands are?

10 Should you stick to one strategy?

Next step

You should now have a good basic knowledge of how to become a better player. In the next chapter you will learn how to get started online. The legality of online poker is discussed, as is how to find an online poker site that is safe to play on. You will also be shown how to play the game online.

8

Getting started online

In this chapter you will learn:

▶ *The history of online poker*
▶ *The legality and fairness of online poker*
▶ *How to find an online site*
▶ *The checks you should make before gambling*
▶ *How to play online poker*
▶ *About solving disputes*
▶ *About chatting to other players.*

What is online poker?

Internet poker (also referred to as online poker) is playing poker via a computer connection over the Internet. Internet poker firms supply computer software via their websites to connect players from all over the world so that they can compete against one an other in a game of poker. The games can be played 24 hours a day, seven days a week, in the privacy of the player's own home.

All types of poker can be played. Online card rooms offer a variety of games including Texas hold 'em, five-card draw, seven-card stud and Omaha. You can play in live games for money or in free games for fun. There are games at all stake levels, starting from $0.01 to no-limit games where you can bet as much as you like. You can also watch games in progress. A wide choice of tournaments is also offered.

For real money games, a rake of typically 1–5 per cent is charged for the use of the poker-room services. The rake is deducted from the winning pot. The rake charged varies with different poker sites. Some offer reduced rates for regular customers. Others may take no rake if, for example, you fold before the flop on Texas hold 'em.

The history of online poker

The first online card room was introduced by Planet Poker in 1998. A year later, in 1999, Paradise Poker arrived and became the industry leader. Today PokerStars is the biggest online poker site with over 50 per cent of the online market. It is licensed by Malta and in other jurisdictions where it operates.

The popularity of online poker is growing year on year. In 2003 there were about 600,000 people playing online. Now it is estimated that approximately 7 million people play Internet poker.

Is online poker legal?

Depending on where you live, Internet betting may or may not be legal. In many countries legislation has yet to catch up with the phenomenon of Internet gambling. Much gambling legislation is outdated. As the legal situation may change at any time, you are advised to check the legality of Internet betting in your jurisdiction before placing any bets. Many countries have realized that they can tax online betting and have started regulating the sites.

In the UK it is legal to play and bet on online poker. The Gambling Act 2005 legislates remote betting. Remote betting includes all types of betting where the parties involved in a bet are not face to face. This includes betting over the Internet, on the telephone and using any future technology that may arise such as betting via a television. The Gambling Act 2005 replaces most of the existing law about gambling in Great Britain. The Gambling Commission was formally established in autumn 2005 and is responsible for controlling gambling by regulating and licensing operators. Licensed gaming sites on the Internet carry a Kitemark to show that the necessary standards have been met. The commission's aim is to keep crime out of gambling, to ensure that gambling is conducted fairly and openly, and to protect children and vulnerable people. Remote gambling software must meet strict technical and security requirements.

Online poker is legal in the European Union (EU). However, individual countries have laws placing restrictions on where players can bet. In 2012 the European Commission adopted the Communication 'Towards a Comprehensive Framework on Online Gambling'. Under European law, obstacles to the free movement of gambling services must be removed. This has resulted in the legalization of online gambling in countries where it was previously banned. France has now legalized online poker and has an online gambling regulator (ARJEL). Italy has also legalized online poker. The European Commission has also started infringement proceedings against several EU states to make them open up their gambling markets to operators from other European countries.

In Australia, the Interactive Gambling Act 2001 prohibits operators from providing online gambling services for real money. In most cases, it is legal for individuals to gamble online. The Australian law has been reviewed with recommendations to allow online poker tournaments. New gambling laws are therefore likely in the near future.

In the United States, the legal situation of online poker has recently been clarified. The Wire Act 1961 is often cited as the appropriate legislation covering Internet betting, but this specifically deals with operating a sports betting business. Case law appears to show that online gambling is legal, but the US Justice Department insisted otherwise. In November 2004 Antigua and Barbuda won a World Trade Organization ruling that United States legislation criminalizing Internet betting violates global laws. In 2006 three major poker sites were prosecuted under the Unlawful Internet Gambling Act of 2006. In 2011 the Department of Justice released a memorandum that concluded that it was legal for states to allow online lottery ticket sales and online gambling. This meant that individual states could allow online poker.

In April 2013 Ultimate Poker became the United States' first legal online poker site. However, it is only legal in Nevada. Other states are also planning to legalize online gambling including New Jersey, Delaware, California, Illinois, Michigan, Connecticut and Pennsylvania.

Remember this: Guidelines for staying legal when playing online poker

* Because the situation is constantly changing, it is necessary to keep up to date with the latest news.
* If you live in an area where Internet poker is not legal, you may find it impossible to get an online card room to accept bets from you.
* There are restrictions placed on age. Although the age of majority may be 18 where you live, you may find that you have to be over 21 to gamble.
* Only play with sites that are legal where you live.
* You may be restricted to playing at certain sites that are licensed by the government. Playing with government licensed sites allows you greater security as there will be controls in place to ensure that the games are fairly played.

Although online betting offers greater convenience to the customer, it does need to be treated with caution as there are a number of scam sites as well as sites that have gone bust owing customers money. Betting on the Internet is a relatively new phenomenon and there is a lack of control and legal framework in some countries to deal with problem sites. If you do play with an unlicensed site and win, they may refuse to pay you out. Recouping any money paid to the site may be extremely difficult or impossible, especially if they operate out of a part of the world with no legal recourse.

Is online poker fair?

Some governments strictly regulate online gambling. In the UK, for example, checks are made into the background of a firm's owners to ensure that they are fit and proper persons. They must demonstrate that they have sufficient funds to pay the players. The software used must be audited to ensure that it is fair. Players' money must be 'ring-fenced' so that it is protected and cannot be used by the firm for running expenses and so on. They are required to run responsible gambling with details of where problem gamblers can get help.

It is advisable to check online forums to see what other players say about a site you are considering playing on. Players are quick to complain if they think they are being conned. Some sites have been accused of manipulating results. Keep up to date as the situation may change. If you can't seem to win with a particular site, cash out and take your custom elsewhere.

The innovation of webcam poker is also helping to give players a sense of fair play, as they can see their opponents. They have the confidence that they are not playing against 'bots' – automated players.

Cheating

Combating cheating has always been a priority for online poker firms. Online poker is vulnerable to collusion. With many games of online poker, because you can't see the other players, you can communicate your hand to another player. It is easy for two players who are friends to communicate while playing, either over the phone or via instant messaging. If the two decide to collude, whichever player has the better hand plays his hand, the other folds. This way they have two chances of getting a better hand. If more players co-operate as a team, then the dupe stands little chance of winning.

It would also be possible for a computer expert to operate a number of computers consecutively and make it appear that several players are competing against one another when in fact all the computers are in one room and he is controlling the action of all the players bar one in a game. In this situation, because he knows all of the hands except that of one opponent, he can play the hands in such a way that the highest-ranking hand always wins.

The online poker rooms are aware of this form of cheating and combat it using software to detect colluders. The software monitors the frequency of two players playing in the same game, unusually high winning rates and suspicious playing patterns such as players folding when they have very good hands. If colluders are caught, they will have their accounts suspended and may lose any money held in their accounts. Their membership of the poker room will be cancelled and details of their cheating may be shared with other gambling sites, which will make it more difficult for them to open another account with a poker room. If you suspect that this kind of cheating has occurred in a game that you have been involved in, you should inform the site.

ALL-IN ABUSE
Some players will try to abuse the all-in rule, disconnecting their computer at a time when it is advantageous to do so. To combat this, sites place limits on the number of times that all-in can be used. If the player is disconnected again, then their hand is automatically folded.

USING SOFTWARE TO AID PLAY
Many software programs that help players to decide the best move are banned. The sites actively look for players who are using banned software. Some software gathers information about players and collates it into a database, but the use of such databases is also not allowed. It is considered that this gives players an unfair advantage. You are allowed to use charts and your own records of information gathered in a conventional manner like making notes as you play.

How to find and assess an online site

The section 'Taking it further' at the back of this book lists major online poker sites. Take your time to check out several sites. They all have different graphics. Some sites are better designed than others. Find the style of layout and cards that you prefer, where it is easy to follow the action.

CHECKS TO MAKE BEFORE GAMBLING

Before depositing any money and gambling, there are a number of checks that you should make. Find out what licensing jurisdiction the site is run under. Don't take the site's word that they are licensed; check with the licensing authority that the site has a legitimate licence. In the UK, Gambling Commission licence holders must display a statement that they are licensed and regulated by the commission along with their licence number. This is often found at the foot of their web pages. You can then check these details against the register of operators on the Gambling Commission website.

Although a site's home page may state that it is regulated in a particular place, you should also check where the poker is regulated, as some gambling products may be regulated in different jurisdictions. A site may, for example, have its horse-racing activities regulated in Britain and its casino games in another country.

Crucial checks to make include the following:

▶ **Check that contact details are clearly given on the site.** You will need to know how to contact the company in case you encounter any problems. Look for a site that gives 24/7 support. This ensures that, if you have any problems, you can contact a member of staff no matter what time of day it is. Make sure that there is a complaints procedure in place. Ideally, there should be a system that refers any disputes to an independent body (like IBAS – see 'Taking it further').

▶ **Read the terms and conditions.** You need to pay particular attention to any conditions for sign-up incentives and bonuses. These can often require that you bet a minimum level of stakes to qualify. Find out how much commission/rake the site takes, as this will vary depending on the stakes. There may also be charges for exchanging currency.

- **Check whether your funds are ring-fenced** (that is, your funds are held in a separate account from the company's funds) – they cannot be seized if a company becomes insolvent.

- **Make sure that the site has a privacy policy.** Ensure that you use a site where personal information is encrypted. As you will be giving personal details, bank account information and credit card numbers to a site, you will want to be sure that this information is securely transmitted and safely held so that it cannot be accessed by a third party.

- **Look for sites that allow you to place limits on the amount that you can deposit or bet.** This will help you to keep a better control on your gambling without going over budget. A responsible site will also have information about what to do if you have a gambling problem. You should be able to exclude yourself from gambling with the site. Responsible sites should also have procedures in place to check that you are of legal age to gamble.

- **Ensure that the site actively checks for colluders and has a policy of barring anyone caught.** Also look for a company that has a policy of limiting the number of all-ins. This will stop cheats taking advantage of the all-in rule.

- **Find out whether the site has a good reputation.** Look for information giving a site's pay-out percentages. You need to ensure that your money is protected and that the games are fair. A poker site should have its card-shuffling software independently audited to check that it is fair.

There are lots of gambling forums on the Internet where gamblers discuss their experiences about online poker. A quick look around Internet forums can alert you to customer complaints. There are also many sites that give blacklists of companies that have failed to pay out or to treat customers fairly. Before depositing any money, you should check that your chosen site is not on any of these lists. Stay away from sites with poor reviews or lots of customer complaints.

> **Remember this:** Keeping safe online
>
> Keep your password secret. Anyone who has access to your password could place bets and withdraw money from your bank account or credit card. If you use a computer that is accessible by more than one person, don't save the password so that it can be automatically entered by the computer. Another person using the computer would be able to access your account.

PHISHING

Phishing is a method used to obtain a player's password to their online poker account. What will generally happen is that the dupe will get an email from the poker site, claiming to be from customer support. They will give some spurious reason why the customer needs to contact them. The dupe will be directed to a web page where it will be necessary to type in his user name and password. The cheater then has the information needed to log in to the dupe's account and bet with the money in the account. The cheater then bets all the dupe's money on a hand where he is head to head with the dupe and all the money from the dupe's account is transferred to his account.

Another method of phishing is to phone or text you. Somewhere within the exchange you will be asked for your password.

Government agencies and poker sites are actively working to combat this fraud. The poker site will often quickly be aware that a fraud of this type is being attempted and will send a warning to members or post a warning on their site. If you get an email claiming to be from the poker site, do not click on any of the links posted in the email. Instead, go directly to the site and log on from the site's home page. If you suspect that you have received a phishing email, report it directly to the site.

HOW TO SOLVE DISPUTES

If a site is government licensed, you can address any complaints about the site to the licensing authority.

In the UK the Independent Betting Adjudication Service (IBAS) offers a dispute settling service. You can refer your problem to them after you have exhausted the site's own complaints procedure.

If a firm is a member of the Interactive Gaming Council (IGC), it is possible to apply to the IGC for mediation if you have a complaint against a member company. The Interactive Gaming Council is a non-profit organization.

How Internet poker works

The online card rooms use computer software to produce virtual card rooms. Players see a depiction of a card table on their screen, showing the other players as avatars or uploaded photo, and details of their own hand, much like what you see on console games. Live webcam games allow you to actually see the other players, of course.

The software uses a random number generator to determine the order of the deck of cards. This ensures that, with each new game, the cards are randomly shuffled. The software deals the cards and prompts the players to make their decisions about their hands. At the appropriate times in the game it gives the options of check, call, bet, raise or fold. These options will appear on the screen. Players select which option they want by clicking with their computer mouse. The screen will tell you how much you need to bet to stay in the game and provide the options that you have at that point in the game. Throughout the game, a running total of the pot and the actions of the other players are shown. At the showdown, the cards of the remaining players will be revealed. The software deducts the amount of the bets from each player's account and credits any winning pots to their account.

Because the games are operated by a computer, they are run at a much faster pace than normal poker games. There is no dealer so there is no time wasted while the cards are shuffled, dealt and collected. Because the cards are not seen until they are dealt, there is no need to 'burn' cards as in a traditional game. There is often a time limit imposed during which you are required to make a decision about your hand. If you do not act within the time limit, then your hand is folded.

The rules tend to be similar to those found in bricks-and-mortar casinos. Owing to the Internet environment there are also special rules that cover what happens if a player gets cut off from the Internet during a game.

How to play

You will need a computer with an Internet connection. The faster your connection the better, because delays in transmission of data can slow down games. With time limits placed on betting, you will need to ensure that your computer quickly communicates your decision.

You will need to find a suitable online poker site. The website addresses of major poker sites are given in 'Taking it further' at the back of this book. Before you can play you will need to sign up for an account. This involves filling in an online form with your personal details. The general requirements are that you are over 18 years of age and live in a place where Internet betting is legal. In some countries you may need to be older. Proof of your age and residence will be required. You will need to ensure that you comply with your own local, national or state laws before opening an account or placing a bet. If you live in an area where Internet gambling is illegal, you may be refused an account.

Registration involves selecting a user name and password, which you will need when logging in to the site. The user name will usually be a nickname that will identify you when you play. You will need an email address so that you can be contacted by the site. Accounts are often available in a choice of currencies so that you will be able to bet in your local currency.

Downloading and installing software

Before you start playing you will need to download and then install software on your computer. The software will run the game programs. A site will typically list the minimum system requirements needed to play their software, including:

▶ the operating systems supported

▶ the download size – how much space you need on your hard disk to install the software and how quickly this will download

▶ the amount of RAM required

▶ the minimum requirements for your modem.

The software keeps records of the hands that have been played. You can look at your hand history. This gives you the opportunity to analyse your game and see where you are going wrong or where you have been successful.

You will have the option to personalize the pages that you see. One of the options is to play with a traditional deck in two colours or with a four-colour deck where the clubs are green and the diamonds are blue or purple. It is advisable to use the four-colour decks because you will be playing on a small screen and the cards appear much smaller than real cards. Distinguishing between hearts and diamonds or spades and clubs is harder. This can make it very easy to mistake a hand for a flush when there is no flush present.

Using a four-colour deck is also advisable for multi-play. If you are multi-playing you will have several tables displayed on your screen, making the card symbols even smaller. The different colours of a four-colour deck make the identification of the hands faster and easier. At first, a four-colour deck takes some getting used to but can save you money in the long run by cutting down on the misidentification of hands.

You will be able to upload a photograph or select an avatar to identify yourself on the site.

The screen can be customized in a number of ways to different colours and table layouts. You will have options to automatically replenish your chips should you be running low. You should play around with the various options until you find a style that you like.

Depositing and withdrawing money

In order to start betting, you will first need to deposit money with the site. Money can be deposited in various ways including credit cards, debit cards, cheques, money orders and so on. For speed, credit cards and debit cards are ideal. They allow you to deposit funds directly and to start betting immediately. With other forms of payment you may have to wait until the money has been received by the site, which can result in a delay of several days before you can start betting.

You can withdraw your money in a number of ways. With some sites your money will be credited back to the source of the money. So, for example, if you deposited money from a credit card, a withdrawal of money will be credited to your credit card account.

The lobby

Hold'em	Omaha	Stud	Draw

Table	Stakes	Type	Players	Avg pot	H/hr
Orange	£1,000/2,000	NL	2/6		
Lemon	£500/1,000	NL	5/9		
Purple	£200/100	PL	0/6		
Green	£100/50	FL	5/9		
Lavender	£5/10	FL	7/9		
Lilac	£1/2	FL	4/9		

Orange £1,000/2,000

Take seat
Take seat
Take seat
Take seat
Take seat
Take seat

Cashier   View table

Figure 8.1 The lobby

The lobby is a multi-purpose page that can take you to various locations on the site. Here you can sign in to your account by clicking on the 'log in' button. Clicking on the 'cashier' button will take you to a screen where you can deposit money and cash out.

The various games of poker available will be displayed. To play Texas hold 'em, you click on the Hold 'em button. You then decide what type of game you want to play – fixed-limit, no limit, pot-limit or a tournament.

Clicking on 'fixed-limit' will bring up a list of games currently available. The stakes will be shown and the number of players. There may also be an indication of the speed of the game. If the game has not yet started, there will be an indication of how long it will be until the game gets under way.

You will often have the option of filtering for your preferred stakes with choices like high, medium, low and beginner. Information like the average pot and hands per hour may also be given.

Clicking on a game will bring up a list of names of the players who are currently playing or waiting to play, their location and how much they have in chips. From this screen you can then click on a button to go to that table. You don't have to play; you also have the option to watch the game.

Each site uses a different layout for their lobby, so it is worthwhile taking your time to familiarize yourself with all the different features and where to find them. Many of the online sites mimic casino play.

You can take a look around and decide which game you would like to join. An information box will tell you the name of the game, the limits and type of game, the blinds, and the buy-in. For each table there will be details of how many players are currently sitting at the table and how many are on the waiting list. Once you have selected to join a game, you will be taken to the table. If there is an empty seat at a table, you click on 'join game' and you will be seated at the table. If there are no empty seats available, you can put your name on a waiting list. If you put your name on the waiting list, you will be notified when a place becomes available. You can specify what stakes you want to play for and how many people you want to play against.

The table

A representation of a poker table is shown with the names of the other players indicated at each of the seats. Depending on the facilities offered, this could be just the name of the player, an avatar or a live webcam video. You can choose where you want to sit from the remaining seats. As soon as the seats are filled the game will begin. The value of the chips each player has will be indicated next to their name. There will often be a chat box where you can talk to the other players. You are not obliged to talk to them.

When the game begins you will be given various options depending on the stage of the game. These will appear as

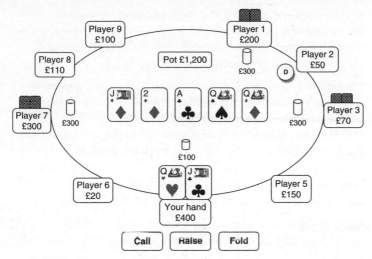

Figure 8.2 The table

buttons that you can click on. If, for example, you wish to bet, you simply click on the 'bet' button. If you wish to fold, you click on the 'fold' button. There will be a time limit for making the decision. This will usually be shown as a graphic counting down the time.

When you first sit down at a table you are prompted to enter the amount of your buy-in. There will be a minimum buy-in that will depend on the game being played.

The players take it in turns to be the dealer. They don't physically deal the cards themselves. All the dealing is carried out by the software. A disc ('dealer' button) will indicate which player is the current dealer.

Your pocket cards will be shown in a prominent position. The community cards are dealt in the middle of the table. The other players' cards will be shown as a graphic of the backs of cards. If they fold, their cards will disappear from the screen. This way you can see who is still in the game. If you fold, your pocket cards will disappear from the screen and the game will be played out without you.

If a showdown is reached, the cards of the players in the showdown will be revealed. The graphics will then show what hand each player holds. This will often be by highlighting the community cards that complete their hands.

The amount of money that each player bets during a game is shown as a graphic of chips with the amount on the table in front of the player. At the end of each betting round the chips are added to the pot. A running total of the pot will be shown. The rake is automatically deducted from the amount in the pot. If you win the pot, the total of the pot will be added to your chip total. You will also see a running total of how much you have left in chips and how much the other players have.

Once all the cards are dealt, the various options that are available during the game will appear on the screen - raise, call, check and fold. If no player has yet made a bet, the option of 'check' will appear. Once a bet has been placed, the subsequent players must call, raise or fold.

You do not have to play continuously. It is possible to take a break, leaving the game for a short while and returning to the same table.

Remember this: What happens if you get disconnected from the Internet?

If you get disconnected from the Internet while a game is in progress, the way that your hand is treated will vary among different sites so you should carefully check the rules. In general, your hand will automatically be played as all-in. If 'check' is an option, the system will check for you. If not, you will go all-in and a separate pot will be created. If you have the winning hand, then you will be awarded the pot that built up at the time that you were disconnected. To avoid abuse of this feature, players are limited to a number of all-ins in a 24-hour period. If you exceed the number of all-ins in that time, your hand will be automatically folded if you get cut off from the Internet again.

Chatting

Players can chat to each other during play by typing messages from their keyboards. Many sites have a code of conduct. Players are expected to be polite when chatting and to refrain from using offensive language. There are restrictions on what you can say. It is forbidden to talk about what is in your hand during a game. Even after you have folded you must not tell other players what you had in your hand until the game is completed. Giving away information about your hand during a game helps the other players to make decisions. You may chat freely once a game has finished. To save time and typing out long sentences, lots of abbreviations are used while chatting. Some of the abbreviation used are shown below.

Chat terms

Writing in capitals or using exclamation marks makes you appear to be shouting.

Ai	all in		mp	middle position
BB	big blind		nb	nice bet
brb	be right back		nh	nice hand
BTN	button		omg	oh my god
C	call		R	raise
Ch	check		SB	small blind
ep	early position		tx	thanks
F	fold		ty	thank you
gg	good game		ul	unlucky
gh	good hand		V-bet	value bet
gp	good play		vnh	very nice hand
gt	got to go		wb	welcome back
hehe	very amusing		wp	well played
lol	laugh out loud		wtg	way to go
lp	late position			

Test your knowledge (answers at the back)

1 What are the minimum stakes you can play real money games for?

2 How much is the rake?

3 What colour are clubs in a four-colour deck?

4 What colour are diamonds in a four-colour deck?

5 Are poker sites monitored for cheating?

6 What will happen if you get cut off from the Internet too often?

7 Are cards 'burnt' as in an offline game?

8 A site states that it is licensed in your jurisdiction. Is it safe to play with them?

9 When playing with a friend, may you give each other information about your hands during the game?

10 Can you use software to calculate your chances of winning?

Next step

You should now be familiar with how to play online, how to find a site and how to check that it is legitimate. In the next chapter you will learn about online tournaments. The different types of tournament available are described, along with tips for how to play.

9

Tournament play

In this chapter you will learn:

▶ *The types of tournament*
▶ *The major tournaments*
▶ *Playing tips.*

What is a tournament?

A poker tournament is a competition between players for prizes. Competing in tournaments is an increasingly popular way to play poker. Texas hold 'em is the most common tournament game as it was chosen to decide the champion in the World Series of Poker. Online sites offer regular tournaments. Many of the highest-paying are held on a Sunday.

Tournaments give players the opportunity to win a large prize for a relatively small entry fee. The more prestigious events attract players with greater skill and pay bigger prizes. For less experienced players there are many tournaments at lower-stake levels.

Tournaments allow players to test their skill against a large field of competitors. A minor tournament may have several hundred competitors. Major tournaments attract several thousand players. This gives players a great deal of experience. You will encounter competitors at various levels of skill ranging from hopeless to highly accomplished.

An advantage of tournaments is that they can be a much cheaper way of playing than regular play, particularly in the minor tournaments. Assuming you get through the initial rounds, an entire day's play can cost the fraction of the price of a regular game. You know in advance how much it will cost. You also have a rough idea of the potential prizes.

Tournament play requires stamina and concentration. With conventional games you can take a break when you like and quit when you are ahead. With tournament play you are there for the duration, which can be up to 14 hours or more in one day. There are breaks allotted but they are short. A typical tournament will allow a five-minute break every hour. The breaks are often synchronized so that players on multi-tables can take a break at the same time.

Types of tournament

There are tournaments featuring fixed-limit, pot-limit and no-limit games. There are two main types of tournament – freezeout (or no-rebuy) tournaments and rebuy tournaments. In both types of game players are eliminated when they lose all of their chips.

NO-REBUY / FREEZEOUT TOURNAMENTS

A freezeout (or no-rebuy) tournament is where players receive an equal amount of chips at the start of the game. They play with this fixed amount of chips until the end of the game. If they get low on chips, they are not allowed to buy more. Players who lose all of their chips are eliminated. If there is a time limit, the winner is the player with the most chips at the end of the competition. In other tournaments play may continue until there is one winner at each table (all the other players have been eliminated). The winners then compete in the next round. Depending on the number of competitors, there may be several rounds to gradually eliminate players. After each round of play, seats are reallocated for the next level. This may be by further draw or may be determined in advance – for example the finalists of table 1 may be scheduled to play the finalists of table 2.

REBUY TOURNAMENTS

In rebuy tournaments players are allowed to purchase extra chips at set points during the game. The amount of the rebuys is usually the same as the initial buy-in. In some tournaments rebuying of chips is unlimited. In others there are limits. The rules may stipulate, for example, that there are two further rebuys allowed. Play continues until players have no remaining chips or for a time limit where the player with the most chips is declared the winner.

PROGRESSIVE STACK REBUY TOURNAMENTS

In progressive stack rebuy games the cost of the rebuy remains constant, but the further you are into the rebuy period, the more chips you get. The effect of this is that the value of the chips decreases as the game continues.

Costs

The costs for entering a tournament comprise the buy-in, rebuys and an entry fee. Minimum buy-ins start from around $15 to $20 and pay prizes of several hundred dollars. Buy-ins for major tournaments are as much as $10,000, with prizes of $1.5 million.

When you see a tournament advertised there is often an entry fee in addition to the buy-in (the minimum amount of chips). An entry fee is typically 10 per cent of the buy-in.

To find the overall cost of a tournament, you will need to total the buy-in, cost of any rebuys and the entry fee. For example: a tournament advertised with a buy-in of $1,000 and an entry fee of $100 will cost $1,100 in total. A tournament advertised with a $500 buy-in and a $50 entry fee with two rebuys of $500 would cost a total of $1,550 if you participate in all the buy-ins.

Entry requirements

Players must be over the minimum age to gamble. This varies depending on local gambling legislation. It is often the age of majority but can be older. Many tournaments are over-subscribed, so it is advisable to register early. At the registration, players pay the amount of the buy-in.

Some major tournaments have particular entry requirements. Players may be required to have won or have been placed in a major tournament. Alternatively, a player may have to compete in a qualifying competition to gain entry. Most tournaments also have separate competitions for women players.

How play is organized

The tournament will be advertised giving the major conditions like the amount of the buy-in, the value and number of rebuys and the entry fee. A set of rules will be available. Play will be scheduled to take place over a certain length of time. Some tournaments last for a few hours; others can take as long as several days.

A random draw is usually held to allocate seats. Players should take up their seats when directed to do so. If you do not arrive on time, your seat may be allocated to another player or, alternatively, you may be disqualified.

Each tournament will have its own set of rules.

If a player runs out of chips during a hand, the all-in rule usually applies. This means that the players can still win the pot to which they have contributed. A second pot is then started for further bets.

Prizes

In some tournaments the prize can be the entry fee to enter a major competition (see Satellites). As well as the prize for the winner, there will often be prizes for several runners-up.

The prizes for most tournaments will depend on how many competitors there are. The value of all the buy-ins is totalled to give the prize money. In tournaments where rebuys are allowed, the value of the rebuys is also contributed to the prize money. The site will often make a deduction for the rake. The majority of the prize fund is awarded to the winner. Several runners-up share the remainder. Some tournaments are winner-takes-all. In some tournaments there will be a guaranteed minimum prize. Often the prize will be more than the minimum. In British tournaments the entire buy-in must be returned as prize money and no additional entry fee can be charged.

Satellites

A satellite is a poker tournament that allows a player to win the stake to compete in a major tournament. For the major tournaments the minimum stake for the finale is high. For example, it may cost $10,000 to enter a tournament. A satellite may be organized for ten players with a $1,000 buy-in. Play continues until there is only one player remaining. The winner receives all of the stake money – that is, $10,000, which is enough to enter the main tournament.

For an even smaller stake, players can enter a super satellite. If they win, it will also give them enough money to buy a seat in the major tournament. In super satellites there is more competition. Players may have to compete in several levels of play to win the stake for the major tournament. In the World Series of Poker, for example, there are super satellites costing $220, which give the players the opportunity of winning the $10,000 needed to enter the major competition. The prize will often include flights and hotel accommodation.

Single-table tournaments are where ten players compete. There is usually a prize for the top three finishers, with the prize being divided as follows:

- ▶ Winner: 50 per cent

- ▶ Second place: 30 per cent

- ▶ Third place: 20 per cent.

In multi-table tournaments you will compete against hundreds of other players. The players will be randomly allocated seats and may play several rounds. As players get knocked out, the remaining players are reseated until just ten players remain on the final table. The winner is the player who wins all of the other player's chips. The advantage of multi-table tournaments is that you can win a large prize for a small entry fee.

SPEED TOURNAMENTS

With speed tournaments the value of the blind increases every few minutes. This ensures that the tournament is quickly finished. Speed tournaments can be played both as single-table games and multi-table games.

SIT AND GO TOURNAMENTS

These start as soon as there are enough players. Blind bets are placed in the player's absence.

MULTI-TABLE TOURNAMENTS

Several tables start off simultaneously. As players are eliminated, the tables are combined until there is just one table remaining.

HEADS-UP TOURNAMENTS

In these, there are just two players per table. The players on each table compete against each other until there is a winner. The winners then go on to the next round to play a winner from another table. The players continue until there is just one winner. A tournament of this type needs to have 2, 4, 8, 16, 32, 64, 128, 256 or 512 players. If there is not a correct number of players in the first round, then some players will be given a bye for the first round and allowed to compete in the second round. These players are allocated at random.

In a heads-up game the players take it in turns to make the small blind and the big blind.

Playing heads-up requires a completely different strategy from games with many players. As you only have one opponent, you will play virtually every hand that you have. You will be winning more pots with much lower-ranking hands than in traditional games. Aggressive play is much more common.

Remember this: Deal making

Sites that allow deal making give players at the final table the opportunity to make a deal for all or part of the remaining prize pool.

Major online tournaments

▶ **World Championship of Online Poker (WCOOP)** Run by PokerStars.com, this is held is September. It is the biggest online tournament with a guaranteed prize pool of $40,000,000. The main event is a $5,000,000 no-limit Texas hold 'em game. Other no-limit hold 'em games offer a $1,500,000 prize pool. Players also win a gold and diamond WCOOP bracelet with travel and accommodation for the presentation ceremony at the Atlantis Resort & Casino in the Bahamas. To enter, players must have a real money account with PokerStars. Satellites start from $1. Qualification is also possible with frequent player points. Buy-ins cost from $215 to $10,300.

▶ **Spring Championship of Online Poker (SCOOP)** This has a prize pot of $40,000,000 and takes place in May. The main event has a buy-in of $10,300. Other games have buy-ins of just $5.50.

▶ **PokerStars Sunday Million** This is a weekly no-limit hold 'em tournament with a $1,000,000 prize pool. It is held every Sunday at 14:30 ET (20:30 CET). First prize is at least

$150,000. A buy-in costs $215. Satellites also take place throughout the week, allowing players to qualify for low stakes. An average of 7,000 players take part.

▶ **888 Poker Sunday Challenge** A weekly tournament with a $100,000 prize pot. Sundays at 19:35 GMT. Buy-in: $82 + $8.

▶ **William Hill Poker**

  ▷ $250,000 Guaranteed Tournament. Every Sunday at 18:00 GMT. Buy-in: $300 + $20.

  ▷ $100,000 Guaranteed Tournament. Every Friday at 19:00 GMT. Buy-in: $100 + $9.

  ▷ $50,000 Guaranteed Tournament. Every Saturday at 19:30 GMT. Buy-in: $100 + $9.

▶ **Party Poker** $250,000 Sunday Guaranteed. Starts 12:45 ET. Buy-in: $215.

▶ **Poker 770** $200,000 tournament from $0.05. Every Sunday at 20:00 ET.

▶ **Absolute Poker** $200,000 Sunday Guaranteed. Every Sunday at 16:00 ET.

▶ **Bodog** $100,000 Guaranteed. Starts Sunday 16:00 ET. Buy-in: $162.

▶ **Full Tilt Poker** $750,000 Sunday Guaranteed. Starts Sunday 17:00 ET. Buy-in: $216.

▶ **Bwin Poker** $250,000 tournament every Sunday.

Remember this: Qualifying for major offline tournaments

It is possible to qualify for major offline tournaments via online contests. Many online poker sites organize contests for the World Series of Poker where players can win the $10,000 entry fee plus accommodation and travelling expenses.

The World Series of Poker

The World Series of Poker is the biggest and longest-running poker tournament in the world. It attracts the elite of poker players. It is held annually at the Rio Hotel and Casino in Las Vegas. Across 30 days, a variety of tournaments are held. Most games take place over two days with play lasting for up to 14 hours in a day. Single-table satellites are held 24 hours a day with buy-ins ranging from $170 to $1,015. Super satellites start from $220. The action culminates in the no-limit Texas hold 'em tournament that takes place over four days. The entry fee is $10,000. The first prize is $1.5 million and membership of the Poker Hall of Fame. The finale is televised around the world.

Strategy for tournaments

▶ Watch lots of tournaments before you start competing. You'll have more confidence if you are familiar with what is going on. Watch the strategy that each player is using and assess its effectiveness. Make notes. It will help you later to remember good strategies.

▶ Make sure that you fully understand the rules and the strategy for the tournament game before you play. Get a copy of the tournament rules and study them carefully.

▶ Ensure that you understand all the jargon associated with poker tournaments. Lots of unfamiliar terms and slang words are used in poker (see Glossary).

▶ Practise the game as much as possible. This doesn't have to cost you any money. You can do this at home. Compete in minor tournaments and gradually work your way up before taking on the professionals. Don't start with major tournaments, as the competition will be the best of the world.

▶ Make sure that you have plenty of sleep and are well relaxed before a tournament. During the tournament you will have to concentrate for around 10–12 hours, which is very tiring. The breaks are extremely short, typically ten minutes every one-and-a-half to two hours. During the break, get some fresh air and stretch your legs.

- Avoid drinking alcohol as it slows down your reactions.

- Keep records of your hands and how you and your competitors played. Analyse your games and how you played. This way you can learn from your mistakes. A diary can be particularly helpful if you play regularly in tournaments. You will often meet the same opponents in competitions. By keeping a log of their strengths and weaknesses, you can improve your chances of beating them.

- Aim to win the top prize. Don't sit back and relax when you know you've reached the prize level. A minor prize will be little more than your original stake.

- Take advantage of the fact that you are playing against strangers. Your competitors in the tournament will know nothing about your method of play or past blunders. Don't be intimidated by your competitors. You may be up against strong competition with seasoned players who have won major tournaments, but each game is different. Play to the best of your ability. It may just be enough to win.

- Learn to quickly assess the other players. Look for their strengths and weaknesses. Even when you're not contending for the pot, closely watch how the other competitors are playing. Be prepared to revise your initial assessments.

- Once you identify weak opponents, play aggressively against them.

- If your game finishes earlier than others, watch the competition. You may gain valuable information about your competitors in the next round.

- Don't waste chips. To stay in a game, it is important to save your chips for your best plays. Unnecessarily staying in for one extra round of betting will cost you a lot of chips. If you have a poor hand and don't intend to bluff, fold early.

- Take advantage of buy-ins. Having more chips allows you to attack more and play aggressively. Being constantly worried about your chip level will make you more cautious.

- If buy-ins of chips are allowed during the game, some players deliberately try to lose chips to participate in the buy-in. If you play aggressively at this time, you can easily accumulate their chips. Your own chip level will also determine whether it is worth losing chips to participate in a buy-in.

- Adapt your play to suit each stage of the game. Play aggressively in the early stages to accumulate chips and intimidate the other players. Some players will be nervous. By appearing confident and by intimidating them with aggressive play, you can push them out of a game.

- It is possible to bluff more than usual. This is because players tend to be more cautious and fold more easily in tournaments. Your assessment of the players will give you a good indication of when to bluff.

- Once you are in a comfortable position with a lot of chips, play more tightly. Save your attacks for your best hands. Let the other players battle among one another.

- Attack players who are low on chips. They are more likely to fold to stay in the game.

- Don't attack aggressive players. Battling with an aggressive player can cost you a lot of chips. Wait until they have folded, then concentrate on attacking the other players.

- Learn to adapt your play to suit the game. If there are several aggressive players at the beginning of the game, let them knock each other out. Once most of the competition has been eliminated, you can start to attack.

- As the number of players drops, you can start to play more loosely and play hands that you may have considered folding with more players. The fewer the number of players, the greater the number of hands you should be playing. When you reach a heads-up situation you should be contesting virtually every hand. This is certainly not a time for tight play, as you will be contributing either the small blind or big blind in every game.

▶ Don't get over-confident. You may be lucky with the draw and have poor competition on the first round but, as you progress to each new level in the tournament, the competition will be tougher.

Test your knowledge (answers at the back)

1 How much will a tournament with a buy-in of £2,000 and an entry fee of £200 cost?

2 How much will a tournament with a buy-in of £100, an entry fee of £10 and two rebuys of £100 cost?

3 On what day do the highest-paying online tournaments take place?

4 How can you win the stake to take part in a major tournament for a small stake?

5 How many players are there in a heads-up tournament?

Next step

In the following chapter you will learn how to keep your gambling under control. You will be shown how to set a budget, to stop you gambling too much. Signs of problem gambling are explained. You will be given advice about what to do if you have a gambling problem.

10

Taking a sensible approach

In this chapter you will learn:

▶ *How to set a budget*
▶ *About exchanging money for chips*
▶ *About the costs of online gambling*
▶ *How to appreciate your chances of winning*
▶ *About online safety*
▶ *How to recognize problem gambling*
▶ *Where to get help with problem gambling.*

Most people are able to gamble in a sensible way without getting addicted or losing too much money. Don't expect always to win. You will have good and bad days. Ideally, you should see gambling as a form of entertainment. Your spending should reflect this and you should spend no more on it than you would on any other form of entertainment. To stop yourself losing too much money, you should set a budget and also determine a time limit for playing. Bear in mind that there are hidden costs to gambling and that online casinos make a profit.

Setting a budget

Before you begin gambling, you should work out a financial budget. Calculate all your household and living costs including savings. Realistically work out how much money you can comfortably afford to lose – yes, lose. Gambling is risky: not everyone wins, and there are plenty of losers. You can easily lose all of your capital. Gambling should not be seen as an alternative to working. Be aware that there are much easier, more profitable and safer ways of making money.

Decide upon a budget that is commensurable with your lifestyle. Once you have decided your budget, make sure you never go over this limit. Split up your budget over the amount of time you expect to gamble. If this is on a daily basis, then you will need to divide your budget by the number of days in a week. If you intend just to gamble once a week, then divide your monthly budget by four. If your personal circumstances change, be sure to recalculate. If you spend only disposable income on gambling, you won't encounter many problems. However, if you start betting with your rent money and lose it, you may be tempted to try to recoup your losses by betting more heavily. This is the route to financial ruin.

Exchanging money for chips

Because you exchange your money for chips, you don't play with 'real money', just a pile of virtual discs. Psychologically, the value of your money diminishes. When you see a banknote, you associate it with its true value – you appreciate how long it would take you to earn that amount of money and what you can buy with it. As soon as you exchange it for chips, those associations disappear. It is no accident that chips resemble coins – coins are considered almost worthless. It's easy to place a pile of chips on a bet. If you had to count out banknotes, you would certainly be more cautious.

When you decide to play, don't immediately change all of your money into chips. Instead, change it in small amounts. If you have to continually go back to exchange your money for more chips, you give yourself the time to change your mind.

If you win, it's all too easy to give your winnings back by continuing to play. Instead, cash in your winnings and take a break.

Online games are played at a much faster pace than traditional games. It is therefore possible to lose your money at a much faster rate. Placing a bet does not even involve the handling of chips. You simply make a click with your computer mouse. Often, there is a time limit placed on how long you have to make a decision. You will be making decisions to bet or raise in a few seconds, which does not allow you the opportunity to give much thought to your decision. As soon as one game is over, the next starts immediately. It is all too easy to continue playing with little thought to how quickly you are losing money.

What does it cost to play?

Once you have calculated your budget, you need to find a game that is compatible with your level of stakes. If the stakes are too high, you will find yourself quickly running out of money.

The minimum amount of capital you need varies depending on the game. Texas hold 'em with fixed limits need around 300 times the minimum stake. No-limit games need considerably more. You can calculate your stake level by dividing the amount that you have budgeted for by the minimum capital required and the number of games you want to play. The minimum stakes on many games are low. You should be able to find somewhere to play to suit your budget. You don't have to be a high roller to play. Most online poker sites have plenty of low-stake tables.

Do not aim too high when you are still learning. Even if your budget allows you to play in the more expensive games, stick initially to the cheaper games and gradually work your way up. Remember, the higher the stakes the better the players.

Online games are played at a fast pace with over 60 hands per hour. This is because the cards are not physically dealt. The hands are dealt by computer software that takes less than a second to deal the cards. This means you can end up playing far more games than you initially intended and consequently bet more money.

Additional costs

It's all too easy to go over your budget by forgetting to include all the costs. Online gambling has additional costs which include such things as:

▶ your time

▶ computer hardware and software

▶ Internet connection

▶ bank fees

▶ the rake/commission charged by the site.

Online poker sites charge gamblers for the use of their facilities. They are, after all, running a business and have to maintain premises, employ staff and buy gaming software and hardware. With poker, a percentage of the pot is taken by the house. This is a small price to pay when you consider that you are guaranteed fairly, professionally run games. Around 1 to 5 per cent is the usual deduction. You should check the sites rule pages to find out exactly how much is deducted. The amount deducted usually depends on the stakes, with different stake levels costing different amounts to play. In general, the higher the stakes the lower the rake. It is worthwhile shopping around to find the lowest rake.

Remember this: Check the rules before you start playing

Remember, the rules can vary from site to site. Ensure that you fully understand all the rules before you play. Learn how to play the game before you bet on it. This may seem common sense, but a lot of people start playing with no understanding of the rules. Often, they are introduced to poker by friends or relations and they simply bet in the same manner as their friends. They end up learning from their mistakes, which can be costly.

Getting plenty of practice

You need to be able to correctly identify a poker hand and recognize immediately the value of your hand and where it comes in the ranking. When you first look at your cards, they will be in a random order and it may not be obvious at first that you have, for example, a straight or a possibility of a straight. At the showdown, you will need to know what beats what – that your full house beats a flush, for instance.

To get better at recognizing the hands, you can practise assessing the hands by dealing out dummy hands. Deal out hands of five cards, identify the poker hands and put them in the correct ranking order. You will soon appreciate how infrequently a good hand is dealt. Once you have mastered the ranking, you can then start to judge whether or not a hand is worth playing. With practice, you will also gain a greater understanding of how extra cards can improve a hand in Texas hold 'em.

Remember this: Get plenty of practice

Take a pack of cards and deal out dummy hands as if you're playing the game with several players. Look at your own hand. Decide whether or not it is worth playing. Then assess your hand against the others. Did you make a good decision? Would any of the other hands have beaten yours? Are you throwing away hands that could easily win? By continuing to do this you will learn the sort of hands that are worthwhile playing and those that are not.

Practise placing bets as you play. Some games are played so quickly that it can be difficult for a novice to follow them. With practice, you will become faster.

As mentioned earlier, it is important to play at the right level. Don't aim too high when you are still learning. Stick to the simpler, cheaper games and gradually work your way up. Remember: the higher the stakes the better the players.

Knowing when to stop gambling

It can take an enormous amount of discipline to stop betting, particularly if you are on a winning streak. It is possible to get carried away by the excitement of the game. You may have intended to spend only an hour gambling, but you're on a winning streak, so you continue. Because you are betting with your winnings rather than the initial stake money, you decide to place larger bets. Your next bet loses – what do you do? For a lot of people the tendency is to bet more heavily to recoup that loss. This will usually continue until you run out of funds.

Here are some tips to help you know when to stop gambling:

▶ If the stakes are getting too high or you are losing too much, stop playing. By having a sensible approach to gambling, you can ensure that you do not lose more than you can afford.

▶ Try to decide in advance at what stage you are going to stop betting. Set yourself an amount to win or lose or impose a time limit. Stop playing when you have reached your limit. As soon as a winning streak stops, either bet small stakes or stop playing. This approach will minimize your losses. Other players may complain if you suddenly stop playing, but remember: you are not betting for their benefit. Do not feel obliged to give them the opportunity to win their money back.

▶ Try setting a time limit. When you start playing, set an alarm clock that will go off after a certain time so that you can keep track of how long you have been playing.

▶ You should always stop playing if you are tired. You need to ensure that you are concentrating on the game. When you are tired, you take longer to make decisions and are more likely to make mistakes.

▶ Don't get angry. Playing in an emotional situation can make you lose money. Don't take revenge on players – this will cost you money.

▶ Avoid alcohol. It tends to slow down your reactions and your ability to think. It also lowers your inhibitions and makes you less likely to care about losses. You should certainly never play if you are drunk.

▶ Ensure that you are concentrating totally on the game in hand. Multi-tasking while playing will distract you and result in you possibly missing vital information that could have helped you to win a game.

▶ It is not unusual to encounter a losing streak. No matter what you do, you just can't seem to win. You play good hands but other players have a hand that just beats yours, or your attempts at bluffing fail. In this situation, take a break from gambling. Take the time to reassess your play and try to attempt to recognize weaknesses. Try to develop a different strategy.

Remember this: Keep records of your gambling

Keep detailed records of your gambling and analyse them after playing. Try to identify your strengths and weaknesses.

How to recognize problem gambling

The majority of gamblers are able to keep to their budgets and bet without it becoming a problem. However, for some people it can become addictive – leading to financial ruin and family breakdown. If you start losing more than you can afford, seek help.

You should keep records of your gambling as this will help you spot whether you are having problems. Keep a diary. Each day note wins and losses. Going back and looking at your track record can help you work out if you are going over budget, rebetting all your winnings or gambling for too long.

You can recognize that you have a problem if you:

► view betting as a way of earning money

► continually exceed your budget

► bet money that was intended for living costs

► borrow money for betting

► take days off work to bet

► spend all your free time betting

► find that your betting interferes with family life.

There are organizations that can offer solutions. Many have a telephone helpline where you speak to a counsellor. They also hold meetings where gamblers can discuss their problems and find solutions. There are also organizations that support the families of gamblers. Your general practitioner will also be able to offer advice on counselling. Details of organizations that can help are given at the end of the book.

Where to get help with problem gambling

Several organizations can help you if you find that your gambling is getting out of control. You can telephone helplines and chat to a counsellor. You can also go along to meetings and discuss your problems with other gamblers.

Some governments and online poker sites also offer self-exclusion schemes. Here you register with the scheme and the online casinos will be notified that you are not allowed to place bets. During the period of self-exclusion they will not take bets from you.

GamCare is a registered charity that is the UK's national centre for information, advice and practical help regarding the social impact of gambling. It gives certification to businesses that implement the GamCare Code of Practice for Remote Gambling. This includes the following practices and features:

- age verification systems

- controls for customer spend

- reality checks within game screens

- self-exclusion options for players

- information about responsible gambling and sources of advice and support

- social responsibility content and sources

- training for customer services in problem gambling and social responsibility.

Details of accredited companies are available on the GamCare website. See 'Taking it further' for contact information for organizations that help with problem gambling.

Checklist before gambling

1 Have your read and understood the rules?
2 Do you understand how to play hold 'em?
3 Have you practised enough?
4 Have you calculated a budget?
5 Have you set yourself a time limit for gambling?
6 Do you have a strategy for playing?
7 Do you understand the odds?
8 Do you know when to quit gambling?
9 Can you recognize the signs of problem gambling?
10 Do you know where to get help with problem gambling?

Glossary

ante a bet made before any cards have been dealt

babies low-value cards

big blind a compulsory bet on the first round of betting

bluff tricking the other players into thinking that you have a really good hand

board the community cards

bullet an ace

button a symbol that denotes the dealer, usually marked with a D

call to match a previous bet

calling station a player who hardly ever raises

chip a disc used in place of money for betting

commission a charge made by the website for its services

community cards the cards placed face up on the table used by all players to make a hand

dead man's hand two pair of aces over 8s

deuce two

flop the deal where the first three community cards are revealed

flush five cards of the same suit

fold withdraw from the game

full house three cards of the same value with a pair; for example three aces and two 6s

hole cards the first two cards dealt to the player

kicker a lower-value card; for example, the hand A, 10 would be referred to as 'an ace with a 10 kicker'

knave a jack

monster a high-ranking hand

nuts having the best possible hand that cannot be beaten

odds a ratio expressing your chances of losing against your chances of winning; odds of 2/1 means you have two chances of losing against one chance of winning

open to place the first bet

over used as a short way of expressing two pair; for example, *queens over 10s* means 'two queens and two 10s'

paint any court card; for example, king, queen or jack

pocket cards the first two cards dealt to the player

poker face having complete control over your facial expressions so that you do not give your opponents any clues about your hand

rake a charge made by the site for their services

river the last community card dealt and the last round of betting

rock a player who always folds unless they have a really good hand

run another name for a straight

see has the same meaning as 'call'

set three cards of the same value

showdown when the players' hands are revealed

stake the amount of money bet

straight five cards of any suit in consecutive order

street a round of betting – the first street is the first round of betting, the second street the second and so on

threes three cards of the same value

trey a three

trips three cards of the same value

Taking it further

Gamblers' help organizations

GREAT BRITAIN
GamCare
2nd Floor
7–11 St John's Hill
London SW11 1TR
Tel: 020 7801 7000
Fax: 020 7801 7033
Helpline: 0808 8020 133
Email: info@gamcare.org.uk
Website: www.gamcare.org.uk

EUROPE

European Gaming and Betting Association
50 rue Gray
1040 Brussels
Belgium
Tel: 32 2 554 0890
Fax: 32 2 554 0895
Email: egba@egba.eu
Website: www.egba.eu

UNITED STATES

Gamblers Anonymous
International Service Office
PO Box 17173
Los Angeles, CA 90017
Tel: (626) 960 3500
Fax: (626) 960 3501
Email: isomain@gamblersanonymous.org
Website: www.gamblersanonymous.org

AUSTRALIA

Gamblers Anonymous
PO Box 122
Fairfield NSW 1860
Tel: (02) 9727 5519
Helpline: (02) 9726 6625
Website: www.gansw.org.au/

Regulatory bodies and arbitration services

Gambling Commission
Victoria Square House
Victoria Square
Birmingham B2 4BP
Fax: 0121 230 6720
Tel: 0121 230 6666
Email: info@gamblingcommission.gov.uk
Website: www.gamblingcommission.gov.uk

Interactive Gaming Council (IGC)
175-2906 West Broadway
Vancouver, BC V6K 2G8
Canada
Tel: 1.604.732.3833
Fax: 1.604.677.5785
Website: www.igcouncil.org

The Independent Betting Adjudication Service (IBAS)
PO Box 62639
London EC3P 3AS
Tel: 020 7347 5883
Fax: 020 7347 5882
Email: adjudication@ibas-uk.co.uk
Website: www.ibas-uk.com

Online poker sites

AllJackpotsCasino.com
Bwin.com
Blue Square.com
Casino.com
Club777.com
Coral.co.uk
888poker.com
Empirepoker.com
FirstWebCasino.com
Galacasino.co.uk
Gamebookers.com
GCasino.com
Getmintedcasino.com
Grosvenorcasinos.com
Jackpotcity.com
Jackpotcitymobile
Jackpotparty.co.uk

Jaxx.com/uk/casino

JFVIPLounge.com

KerchingCasino.com

Lady Luck's Mobile Casino

LesACasino.com

Lucky247.com

Lucky247 Mobile

Mansion Poker.com

Mecca Games.com

Mfortune Mobile Casino

MoobileGames

Mybet.com

PaddyPower Poker.com

PaddyPower Mobile

PartyPoker.com

PKR Poker.com

Platinumplay.com

PokerStars.com

Pokertime.eu

Royalvegas.com

Sky Poker.com

Sportingbet.com Poker

Sportingbet.com Mobile

Stanjames.com

SuperCasino.com

WildJackCasino.com

Wild Jack Mobile

Virgin Poker.com

Answers

Chapter 1

1 One pair – a pair of jacks: Jc, Jd, Kh, 9d, 8d

2 A royal flush/straight flush: Ad, Kd, Qd, Jd, 10d

3 Four of a kind: 8d, 8h, 8c, 8s, Ac

4 A flush: Kc, Qc, 10c, 7c, 3c

5 Highest card: Ac, Kd, Qs, 10h, 8d

6 Two pair – 10s and 5s: 10h, 10d, 5d, 5s, 8h

7 Full house – kings over queens: Kc, Kd, Ks, Qc, Qh

8 Straight: Jc, 10s, 9c, 8h, 7d

9 Three of a kind/trips/set: Qs, Qd, Qh, Kc, Jd

10 A straight flush: 5d, 4d, 3d, 2d, Ad

11 *a* – a flush (five non-consecutive diamonds) – Ad, Kd, Qd, 7d, 4d – beats three of a kind (three kings) – Kd, Kh, Ks, Ah, 7d.

12 *b* – two pair 10s over 4s beats a pair of kings.

13 *b* – a full house queens over kings beats a straight.

14 *a* – a royal flush (Ah, Kh, Qh, Jh, 10h) beats a flush (Ah, Qh, Jh, 10h, 9h).

15 *b* – a full house (10d, 10h, 10s, 7d, 7c) beats a flush (10d, 9d, 8d, 7d, 6d). (But not a straight flush)

16 *a* – a flush (five consecutive diamonds) – Jd, 10d, 9d, 8d, 7d – beats a straight (five consecutive cards of any suit) – Jd, 10h, 9d, 8d, 7d

17 *a* – three of a kind (three jacks) – Js, Jh, Jc, As, Kd – beats two pair (aces and kings) – As, Ah, Kd, Kc, Jh.

18 *a* – highest card (king) – Kd, Jh, 10c, 8s, 6d – beats highest card (queen) – Qd, Jh, 10c, 8s, 6d

19 *b* – a straight (five consecutive cards of any suit) – Qd, Jh, 10c, 9d, 8s – beats three of a kind (three queens) – Qc, Qs, Qd, Jh, 10c.

20 *a* – four of a kind (7d, 7h, 7c, 7s, Ah) beats a full house (Ah, Ac, As, Kd, Kh).

Chapter 2

1 A pair of kings: Kh, Kc, As, Qd, Jc

2 A straight: Qd, Js, 10c, 9d, 8c

3 Four of a kind: Jh, Jd, Jc, Js, 10 (the suit of the ten makes no difference to the hand)

4 A flush (five hearts): Ah, 10h, 9h, 7h, 4h

5 Two pair: Kd, Ks, Qd, Qc, 8s

6 A royal flush: Ac, Kc, Qc, Jc, 10c

7 Three of a kind/trips: Qc, Qd, Qs, Ah, Js

8 Highest card queen: Qc, Jd, 10d, 9h, 7h

9 A straight flush: 10d, 9d, 8d, 7d, 6d

10 A full house jacks over 10s: Jc, Jd, Jh, 10s, 10c

11 *Player a* – a full house aces over 6s (Ac, Ad, Ah, 6c, 6d) beats a full house sixes over aces (6c, 6d, 6h, Ad, Ah).

12 *Player b* – a flush (10s, 8s 7s, 6s, 5s) beats three of a kind/ trips (Kc, Kh, Kd, 9d, 7s).

13 *Player a* – two pair, kings and queens (Ks, Kc, Qs, Qc, Js) beats a pair of aces (Ac, Ad, Kc, Qc, Js).

14 *Player b* – four of a kind (Jc, Js, Jh, Jd, Qc) beats a straight (Ks, Qc, Jh, 10s, 9c).

15 *Player a* – a straight flush (Kd, Qd, Jd, 10d, 9d) beats a flush (Ad, Kd, Jd, 9d, 7d)

16 A tie – the pot is split. Player a has three of a kind with jacks (Jc, Js, Jd, Ad, Kc). Player b also has three of a kind with jacks (Jh, Js, Jd, Ac, Kc).

17 A three-way tie – the pot is split between all three players. Player a has a straight (Ad, Kd, Qd, Jd, 10s). Player b has a straight (Ac, Kh, Qh, Jd, 10s). Player b has a straight (Ad, Ks, Qh, Jd, 10s).

18 A three-way tie – the pot is split between all three players. Each player has a straight flush (Qd, Jd, 10d, 9d, 8d). The community cards are the highest hand.

19 Players a and c tie. The pot is split between players a and c. Player a has four of a kind with four aces and king kicker (Ah, As, Ad, Ac, Kc). Player b has four of a kind with four aces and queen kicker (Ah, Ac, Ad, Ac, Qc) and player c has four of a kind with four aces and king kicker (Ah, Ac, Ad, Ac, Ks). Player a and c have the same hand. Player b's hand is lower because the kicker is a queen.

20 A three-way tie – the community cards are the highest hand (10s, 9c, 8d, 7s, 6d, 5c).

Chapter 3

1 a) £0.50 b) £1

2 a) £2.50 b) £5

3 a) £50 b) £100

4 a) £2 b) £4

5 a) £10 b) £20

6 a) £1 b) £2

7 £10

8 £5

9 £2

10 £100

11 Player 4 makes the small blind; player 5 makes the big blind.

12 Player 6 makes the small blind; player 7 makes the big blind.

13 No – a player can only check if no other player has made a bet.

14 £5

15 maximum raise = call + pot = £120; total bet = raise + call = £140

16 maximum raise = call + pot = £250; total bet = raise + call = £300

17 maximum raise = call + pot = £290; total bet = raise + call = £330

18 £40

19 £200 – you can only bet up to the maximum of your chips.

20 £250 – he can only compete for the pot that he contributed to. He dropped out of the betting at the flop. The fact that his hand is the highest at the showdown is irrelevant for the second pot.

Chapter 4

1 Two kings can be dealt in six ways:

$$\frac{4 \times 3}{1 \times 2} = 6$$

From 52 cards, 1,326 two-card hands can be dealt:

$$\frac{52 \times 51}{1 \times 2} = 1,326$$

$$\frac{1,326}{6} = 221.$$

The odds against getting pocket aces are therefore 220/1.

2 One – there is just one jack left in the deck.

3 Nine – there are 13 hearts in the deck. Four have been dealt, leaving nine.

4 7.5/1 – there are 50 cards left in the deck. These can be dealt in the following number of ways:

$$\frac{50 \times 49 \times 48}{3 \times 2 \times 1} = 19,600$$

There are two cards that could be used to make the three of a kind. That leaves 48 other cards in the deck. They can be dealt in the following number of ways:

$$\frac{48 \times 47 \times 46}{3 \times 2 \times 1} = 17,296$$

The number of three-card combinations that could contain one king is:

$$19,600 - 17,296 = 2,304$$

$$\frac{17,296}{2,304} = \frac{7.5}{1}.$$

5 18 $9 \times 2 = 18$

6 Eight

7 Four

8 No – you are having to bet 25 per cent of the pot with just a 4-per-cent chance of making the hand.

9 The pot odds are 25/5, or 5/1. The odds of reaching the desired hand are 4/1. It is therefore worth betting.

10 The pot odds are 100/10, or 10/1. Your odds of getting the desired hand are 20/1 against. It is not worthwhile betting.

Chapter 5

1 No – at this stage you don't know how many players are going to stay in. You may end up with a lot of competition for the pot.

2 No – there is too much competition.

3 Yes – there is little competition.

4 Yes – you can use this to your advantage as other players may assume you have a lucky streak.

5 Yes – you are coming across as a tight player and it will be assumed by the other players that you have a good hand.

6 No – low-stakes games will often go to the showdown because it does not cost the players very much money.

7 Yes – players will be more cautious in high-stakes games.

8 Yes – players tend to play more cautiously in the early games of a tournament as they try to accumulate chips.

9 No – if there are high cards in the flop it is highly likely that one of the other players will have a match.

10 Yes – spotting a tell gives you an advantage. You can then bet aggressively against this player and force him to fold.

Chapter 6

1 Play

2 Fold

3 Play

4 Fold

5 Play

6 Play

7 Fold

8 Play

9 Play

10 Fold at an early position and play at a late position as a semi-bluff.

11 Play. The hand is the highest visible – three of a kind with 10s.

12 Play. The hand is already three of a kind with little opposition.

13 Play. Although the flop has not helped your hand, it is highly unlikely to have helped anyone else.

14 Fold. There is no chance for a flush. There is likely another player with three aces or at least two pair.

15 Play. You currently have nuts.

16 Yes – no one else is showing strength. It is not costing you much so you may as well continue to the river.

17 Yes – you need to force out other players who could improve on the last two cards.

18 Fold. Your bluff has not worked. Better to fold than to have your bluff revealed.

19 No – he has to bet just 16 per cent of the pot and has a 35-per-cent chance of making the hand.

20 Yes – he now has to bet 44 per cent of the pot and has only a 35-per-cent chance of making the hand.

Chapter 7

1 Fixed-limit

2 No – you should only play your best hands.

3 More loosely

4 A tight player

5 Yes – you will be paying a blind bet in every game.

6 No – you should concentrate on one game at a time as a beginner.

7 No – an ace with a low kicker is not a good hand.

8 More likely

9 Yes.

10 No – varied play is better.

Chapter 8

1 1c

2 1 to 5 per cent

3 Green

4 Blue or purple

5 Yes.

6 Your hand will be folded.

7 No.

8 No – you should check the licensing authority's site to check that this information is true.

9 No – this is collusion and considered cheating.

10 No – many types of software are banned.

Chapter 9

1 £2,200

2 £310

3 Sunday

4 By entering a satellite

5 Two

Index